Simply fabulous clothing and accessories

weave * knit * wear

for rigid-heddle *(and other)* weavers

BOOKS

PUBLISHER • Alexis Yiorgos Xenakis

EDITOR • Elaine Rowley

MANAGING EDITOR • Karen Bright

TECHNICAL EDITOR • Rick Mondragon

PROOFERS • Traci Bunkers • Sarah Peasley

ART DIRECTOR • Natalie Sorenson

PHOTOGRAPHER • Alexis Yiorgos Xenakis

STUDIO PHOTOGRAPHER • Lisa Mannes

STYLISTS • Lisa Mannes • Rick Mondragon

CHIEF EXECUTIVE OFFICER • Benjamin Levisay

DIRECTOR, PUBLISHING SERVICES • David Xenakis

TECHNICAL ILLUSTRATOR • Carol Skallerud

PRODUCTION DIRECTOR & COLOR SPECIALIST • Dennis Pearson

BOOK PRODUCTION MANAGER • Carol Skallerud

MARKETING MANAGER • Lisa Mannes

BOOKS DISTRIBUTION • Molly Bonestroo

MIS • Jason Bittner

FIRST PUBLISHED IN THE USA
IN 2014 BY XRX, INC.

COPYRIGHT © 2014 XRX, INC.

All rights reserved.
ISBN 13: 9781933064291

Produced in Sioux Falls, South Dakota by

XRX, Inc.
PO Box 965
Sioux Falls, SD
57101-0965 USA

605.338.2450

Visit us online — knittinguniverse.com

Simply fabulous clothing and accessories

weave * knit * wear

for rigid-heddle *(and other)* weavers

by **Judith Shangold**

photography by
Alexis Xenakis

MY LIFE IN YARN

In 1975, I was a weaver in search of a way to make a living. I opened a craft and yarn shop in the Park Slope section of Brooklyn, NY, called The Weaver's Studio, offering classes in knitting, crochet, weaving, basketry, and macrame. It was a great time to be in the fiber world. Fiber artists such as Lenore Tawney, Sheila Hicks, Ed Rossbach, and Walter Nottingham were making names for themselves and having their work shown in major art museums. Perry Ellis was designing fabulous handknit sweaters, and knitters were knocking themselves out copying them. New yarns were exploding onto the scene. This was not my mother's yarn world anymore.

I had learned how to knit as a teenager and became re-engaged with yarn in the late '60s, after college. Crochet was popular at the time, and I remember the crazy-quilt throw I attempted, creating blocks of many colors and shapes and crocheting them together. But I had a lot more to learn about knitting and crochet. I taught myself to knit a cable from a book, because asking someone would have been embarrassing—I owned a yarn shop, after all! When I learned something from a customer one day, I taught it to another the next. Before I knew it, I was designing sweaters for the shop.

One of my customers was the editor of *McCall's Needlework & Crafts*, and she suggested that I submit some designs to the magazine. I did, they were published, and first time out, I made the cover! Over the years, I had many designs published in *Vogue Knitting*, *Family Circle*, *Woman's Day*, and *Knitter's Magazine*, and I also designed for yarn companies including Rowan, Bernat, JCA/Reynolds, Manos del Uruguay, Classic Elite, and Crystal Palace.

When I closed the shop in 1985 and moved to the Boston area, my loom was folded up and sent to the basement. I became the New England sales representative for several yarn companies, and also began designing sweaters for bears and dolls under the name "A Bear in Sheep's Clothing." Other patterns for humans followed, under the name "Designs by Judith." My mission was to publish patterns for classic designs that you could make in several gauges, with any yarn. I hoped they would answer the question every yarn shop owner feared: "Do you have a pattern for a simple sweater that I can make with this yarn?"

Fast forward 14 years and add many thousands of miles to the car. It was the beginning of the new millennium. The U.S. importer of Manos del Uruguay, one of the yarns I'd been representing, was retiring from the business. I felt that everything I'd learned about designing and the industry had brought me to this moment, and I bought the business from her. Now I had the opportunity to develop the colors and designs for a yarn I had always loved to weave, to knit, and to sell. It was a wondrous challenge!

By 2005, I started to notice a change in what people wanted to knit. Ready-to-wear had become more fitted, and big, bulky sweaters were becoming less popular. I, like so many others, had knit many sweaters that no longer felt right—they were too big, too shapeless. But the idea of knitting something that really had to fit, and to work with the thinner yarns required to get the right look, was daunting. Accessories had become the rage—felted bags, funky scarves, shawls, wraps, ponchos, throws—things that didn't have to fit. This presented a whole new design challenge. I started looking to designers such as Eileen Fisher for inspiration. I liked the simplicity and easy drape of her clothing, and her new and interesting constructions. I started trying to interpret these ideas into knit designs.

In 2007, I sold the Manos distributorship and returned to weaving. The big, 40-year-old floor loom had to go — there was simply no room in my little house. I started working on a rigid-heddle loom and found that everything I had learned about clothing design from knitting was now informing my weaving. I still wanted easy shapes that didn't require a lot of cutting and sewing — I was not a seamstress — but neither did I want to wear something that looked like a box, and so I continued my exploration into shapes that were simple to make and materials and construction that provided the right drape.

Throughout history, weavers around the world have created clothing for protection, adornment, and social approval. If one studies the clothing from earlier civilizations, a common theme emerges. An Egyptian tunic from 1400 BC, a Roman toga from 100 AD, a Japanese kimono from the fifth century AD, a Guatemalan huipil from the 1700s, and a Mexican serape from the 1800s all have one thing in common: They were created from rectangular pieces of handwoven cloth.

In my quest for easy-to-make and easy-to-wear garments, this was a natural place to begin. I wanted to take it a step further though, to create garments that were a little more fashion forward. I started to think about the possibilities of combining weaving and knitting. Each has its own positive attributes. Woven fabric has a wonderful drape, and working with finer yarns is less daunting; you can weave many more inches in an hour — even with the thinnest yarns — than you can knit. With knitting, you can shape pieces such as sleeves, armholes, and necklines without having to cut and finish edges, and knit fabric is more elastic — it will stretch to fit the body's shape. Start with a woven rectangle, add knitted side panels, gussets, collar, or sleeves, and voila! It's not a box anymore.

And so we come to this book. It is not the end of the story, but rather the beginning. Weaving is becoming ever more popular among fiber enthusiasts. There are wondrous new fibers like bamboo, soy, and tencel that mimic the drape and feel of silk at a fraction of the cost. We have the Internet, Ravelry, and Project Runway to inspire us. If you are a knitter and haven't considered weaving, I hope these projects inspire you to try it!

I created all of these garments on a 20" wide rigid-heddle loom. This simple device allows the weaver to create a continuous length of cloth in a plain-weave structure. All of my garments are created from pieces that are 18" wide or less, mostly using knitting yarns from fingering to aran weight. The directions are given for creating the garments as I did on a rigid-heddle loom.

If, however, you are an experienced weaver with a larger, multi-harness loom, there are no limits to what you can produce with your equipment, your materials, and your creativity. I invite you to explore the styles I have presented and to create your own masterpieces.

TABLE of CONTENTS

weave • knit • wear

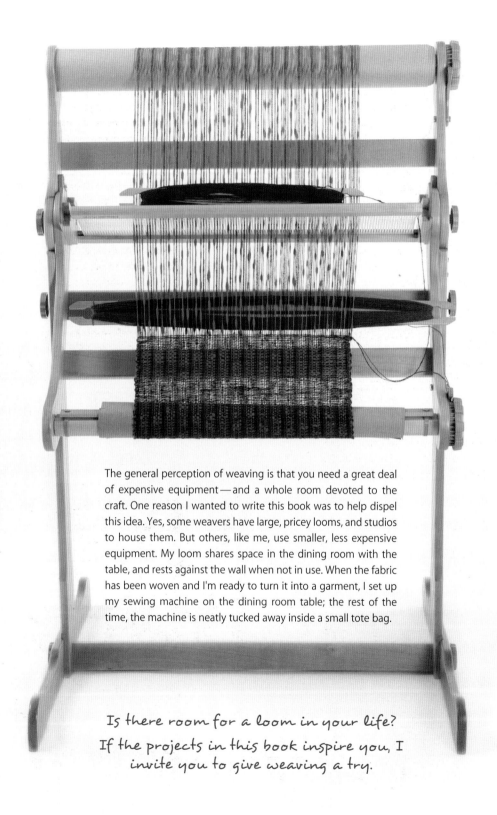

The general perception of weaving is that you need a great deal of expensive equipment—and a whole room devoted to the craft. One reason I wanted to write this book was to help dispel this idea. Yes, some weavers have large, pricey looms, and studios to house them. But others, like me, use smaller, less expensive equipment. My loom shares space in the dining room with the table, and rests against the wall when not in use. When the fabric has been woven and I'm ready to turn it into a garment, I set up my sewing machine on the dining room table; the rest of the time, the machine is neatly tucked away inside a small tote bag.

Is there room for a loom in your life? If the projects in this book inspire you, I invite you to give weaving a try.

WEAVING TOOLS
LOOMS

A loom with 4 or more **shafts** (also called harnesses) allows you to weave textiles with structures ranging from simple to very complex. With a 2-shaft loom, you can do **plain weave**. This is the most basic of woven cloth constructions, and is achieved by weaving over a **warp** thread, under the next, over the next, and so forth. One type of 2-shaft loom is a **rigid-heddle loom**. Every other warp thread is threaded through a hole in the heddle. Since the heddle is rigid, it lifts and lowers the hole threads when it is raised and lowered, forming the 2 openings (the **sheds**) needed for plain weave.

Mainly due to limited space, this is the type of loom I currently have, and the loom with which I have made all of the projects in this book. Some weavers use a rigid-heddle loom to create more complex weaves by using multiple heddles and **pick-up sticks**. I choose to use 1 heddle, and only occasionally a pick-up stick. Let's just say I like to keep things simple. When knitting, I am partial to garter, stockinette, seed, and slipped stitches. I am more interested in challenging myself with color and design.

A rigid-heddle loom is a great way to begin your adventure in weaving. As you will see, the possibilities, even with this simple piece of equipment, are limitless. The widest loom required for the projects in this book is 20". Some of the projects don't require more than 12" (see the Project Index on page 137). The reason for this is that most of the garments are made in pieces that are sewn together to achieve the desired width. If, however, you are in the market for a loom and clothing is your main interest, consider the sleeve. A sleeve is generally made in 1 piece, and for larger sizes (anything over a medium) the finished width at the top of the sleeve needs to be 18–22"—this would require a minimum loom width of 24". In this book, I have shown some creative ways of achieving this width by adding knit gussets, but this is not always a desirable alternative.

A rigid-heddle loom can be used up against a table with one end sitting in your lap, but I prefer to use mine on a stand. This frees me to use the loom wherever I want, and to turn it in any direction to get the best light. An added advantage is its portability; without the stand, the Ashford Knitters Loom and Schacht Flip Loom can be folded up (even when warped), put in a bag, and taken with you.

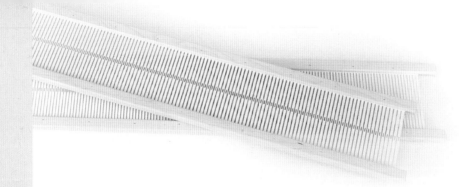

Front apron rod

After winding the warp, then pulling 1 end from a slot and threading it through a hole, the warp threads get tied on here.

Fulling

The result of wet finishing a fabric, causing the fibers to bloom, cling to each other, and shrink. The degree of shrinkage depends on the amount of heat and agitation used.

Heading

Prior to weaving the actual fabric, the heading is woven with waste yarn, toilet paper, or cardboard strips to spread the warp threads evenly.

Heddle hook

A special hook used for pulling loops through slots and threads through holes.

Pick

A row of weft.

Pick-up stick

A flat, pointed stick used to pick up groups of warp threads.

Plain weave

The simplest weave in which the weft passes over and then under warp threads in the first pick and then reverses that path (under and then over) in the second pick. These 2 picks are repeated throughout.

PPI

Picks per inch.

Reed

The part on a multi-shaft loom through which the warp ends are threaded. It corresponds, in part, to the heddle on a rigid-heddle loom.

HEDDLES

Rigid-heddle looms are available with different-sized heddles — 5, 8, 10, and 12. The number refers to the number of openings (slots and holes) or **dents** (a useful term from the shaft-loom world that refers to the spaces in a **reed**) per inch, or **dpi**. Note that some of the looms have metric-sized heddles that are 7.5 or 12.5 dents per inch. The heddle required is determined by the weight of the yarn you are using and the density of the fabric you wish to achieve. A thinner yarn requires a higher number of warp threads (or **ends**) per inch, or **epi**. I have used 3 different heddle sizes: 7.5/8, 10, and 12/12.5 (see the Project Index on page 137).

SHUTTLES

Shuttles hold the yarn for weaving. Rigid-heddle looms generally come with a couple of stick shuttles; you will probably want extras, as you will need one for each color you are using for a project. I prefer shorter ones, no longer than 12", as they are easier on my arms and shoulders.

You might also want to consider purchasing a boat shuttle. These are a little costly, but I believe they are worth the investment, especially when working with finer yarns. You may want 2 of them since, for many of the woven patterns shown, you are working with 2 colors at the same time. Look for small, narrow boat shuttles if working on a rigid-heddle loom.

BOBBINS AND BOBBIN WINDER

If you decide to purchase boat shuttles, you will also need bobbins and a bobbin winder. A bobbin winder is a tool that makes winding a bobbin fast and easy. You will want several bobbins; they are generally sold in bags of 10 or so.

OTHER USEFUL EQUIPMENT

SWIFT AND BALL WINDER
Many yarns come in skeins. A swift will hold the skein while you wind it into a ball by hand or with a ball winder, or wind it onto a bobbin with a bobbin winder.

TAPESTRY BEATER
If you are going to try tapestry technique (see page 26), you will need a beater. This can be as simple as a kitchen fork, but there are some beautiful wooden beaters available. Most are made to be heavy, with wooden teeth, for weaving rugs. The one I use for working on lighter, more delicate material has a wooden handle and metal prongs.

SCALE
A scale is useful for weighing yarn if you don't have full skeins. Look in an office supply store for a digital postal scale that weighs in both ounces and grams. If you know the original yardage per skein, divide that number by the original weight of the skein—this will tell you the number of yards per ounce or gram. Now weigh the yarn you have and multiply the weight times the yards per ounce or gram. If your 100g skein originally had 200 yds, then 1g = 2 yds. If you now only have 50g, then you have 100 yds.

PICK-UP STICK
A pick-up stick is used for doing some hand-manipulated lace techniques and pick-up patterns on the rigid-heddle loom. It can also be useful if your warp is sticky. If that is the case, open a shed by raising or lowering the heddle, then slip the pick-up stick into the shed behind the heddle. Push it all the way to the back of the loom and leave it there.

Rigid heddle
A rigid tool with alternating slots and holes that raises and lowers the hole threads to form the sheds for weaving.

Selvedge
The side edge of the weaving.

Shaft (harness)
A frame used to raise and lower warp threads.

Shed
The opening that develops when the heddle or a combination of shafts are raised or lowered.

Shuttle
A tool that carries the weft through the shed. There are several varieties, including stick and boat.

Sley
The action of pulling the warp threads through the heddle or reed.

Warp
The vertical threads of a weaving.

Warp beam
The beam at the back of the loom around which the unwoven warp threads are wound and released for weaving.

Warping board
A tool used to measure the warp threads prior to setting up the loom.

Warping peg
Used for measuring warp threads when direct warping.

Weft
The horizontal threads of a weaving.

WARPING A RIGID-HEDDLE LOOM

If you are working on a rigid-heddle loom, I highly recommend the **Direct Warping** method, which eliminates the need for a **warping board**. In Direct Warping, you tie the yarn to the **back apron rod** and pull loops through the slots of the heddle with a **heddle hook**. Once all of the required slots are full, the warp is wound onto the **warp beam**. Loops are then cut in front of the heddle, leaving 2 threads in each slot. One thread is removed from each slot and pulled through the hole next to it.

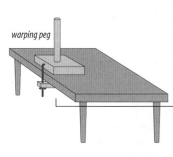

warping peg

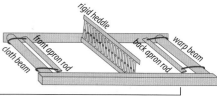

1 Set up loom with warping peg placed desired distance from back apron rod.

rigid heddle

front apron rod

back apron rod

warp beam

cloth beam

length of warp

All of these possibilities are explored within the patterns, with specific directions provided.

For a striped warp, pull through as many loops as desired with color A. Cut the yarn and tie it to the back apron rod. Tie color B to the back rod and pull through as many loops as desired. Continue across, always starting and ending colors at the back apron rod.

To alternate colors, tie both onto the back apron rod. Pull a loop of color A through a slot, then pull a loop of color B through the next slot. Continue to alternate across. Once you have threaded the holes, the result will be 2 threads of color A followed by 2 threads of color B.

To alternate a thread of 1 color with a thread of another, pull a loop of color A through a slot and a loop of color B through a hole. Skip the next slot and hole. After the warp is wound onto the back beam and the loops are cut, pull 1 thread from a slot through the empty slot next to it; pull 1 thread from a hole through the empty hole next to it. The result is that all color A threads will be in slots and all color B threads will be in holes.

Log cabin uses a variation of this method. Color A is in slots and color B is in holes for 1 section, then the colors switch, with A in the holes and B in the slots for the next section. By alternating these 2 sections and weaving the weft in a similar fashion, you can create interesting, very complex-looking patterns. Even more interesting effects happen if one of the yarns is thick and the other thin.

If you want to use a fine yarn doubled, pull a loop through a slot and then pull a loop through the hole next to it. Two threads will remain in each slot and hole. Each doubled warp thread is referred to as 1 *working* warp thread.

A method for warping with 3 or more colors in a pattern, or for using colors in a random fashion, is to tie on 1 color and thread it through the desired slots—let's say every third slot. When finished, cut the thread and tie it to the back apron rod. Then take the next color, pull it through slots as desired, and tie it off. Continue across with as many colors as desired.

A lacy, openwork look can be achieved by leaving some slots and holes unthreaded.

weave • knit • wear

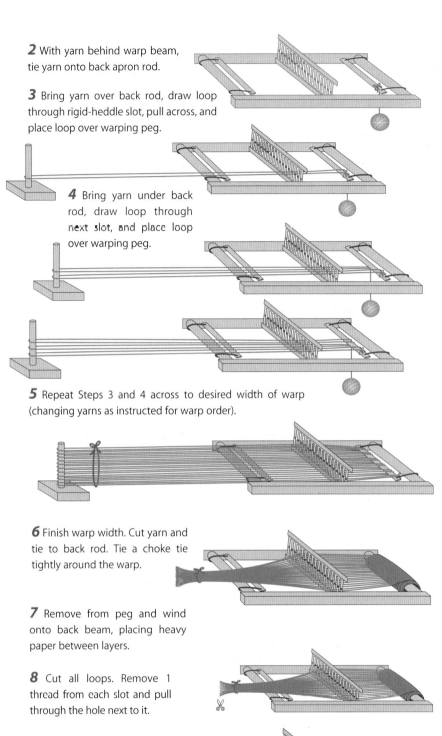

2 With yarn behind warp beam, tie yarn onto back apron rod.

3 Bring yarn over back rod, draw loop through rigid-heddle slot, pull across, and place loop over warping peg.

4 Bring yarn under back rod, draw loop through next slot, and place loop over warping peg.

5 Repeat Steps 3 and 4 across to desired width of warp (changing yarns as instructed for warp order).

6 Finish warp width. Cut yarn and tie to back rod. Tie a choke tie tightly around the warp.

7 Remove from peg and wind onto back beam, placing heavy paper between layers.

8 Cut all loops. Remove 1 thread from each slot and pull through the hole next to it.

9 Tie onto front apron rod.

or

WARPING TIPS FOR RIGID-HEDDLE LOOMS

- When calculating the length of your warp, you must allow for loom waste. I have allowed 24" for the projects in this book, all worked on a rigid-heddle loom. For other looms, you may need to add more length. A floor loom might require as much as 36" of loom waste.

- If you have a stand for your loom, you can use it while you are warping. Attach the **warping peg** to a table or stool and place the loom on its stand, as far from the peg as necessary to achieve the desired warp length. Place some weight on the bottom of the stand to keep it from slipping forward while you are warping. For warping purposes, it's best for the loom to remain horizontal. If it tips forward on the stand, place a stool or chair under the front edge of the loom to hold it in place.

- To achieve the widest warp possible, place the first loop to the outside of the heddle. The last loop will be in the last slot of the heddle.

- If warping your loom for a warp wider than 6", wind the warp in sections. Align the peg with the right side of the heddle and wind about a third of the warp. Tie a piece of yarn tightly around the warp threads (**choke tie**) and remove the threads from the peg. Move the loom so the peg is now aligned with the center portion of the heddle and wind the next portion of the warp. Tie a choke tie and remove the threads from the peg. Repeat for the last portion of the warp, aligning with the left side of the heddle. This will help maintain an even length for all of the warp threads.

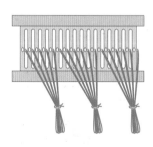

- Wind the warp onto the back warp beam using heavy paper to separate the layers.

- When winding on, adjust the tension on the warp threads, a small section at a time, after every few turns of the back beam.

WEAVING TIPS

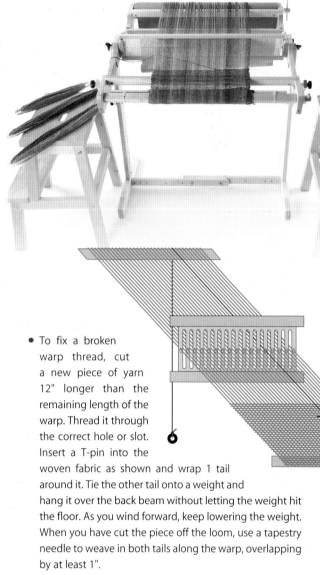

- I like having a table, chair, or stool on either side of my rigid-heddle loom while I am weaving. This provides places to put my shuttles, scissors, tape measure, note pad, etc.

- I start weaving with toilet paper (you can also use a heavy, smooth, scrap yarn), weaving as many strips as necessary to evenly spread the warp. This is called the **heading**.

- The tension on the warp threads should be even across the loom. After you weave a few **picks** with the **weft** you are using for the project, the fell of the cloth (the path taken by the last warp thread you have inserted) may become uneven. If the fell dips toward you, the warp threads there are too tight. If the fell curves toward the heddle, the threads there are too loose. Untie the knots from the **front apron rod** and adjust the tension as needed.

- Weaving in tails: To start a new color, leave the weft tail hanging at the **selvedge** while you weave the first row. **Beat** and change sheds. Weave the tail into the shed, then bring the shuttle across for the next row.

- To end a color, cut the yarn and, wrapping the tail around the last warp thread, weave it back into the same shed as the last row of weaving.

- Aim for an even beat — not too tight, not too loose — and a balanced weave. For example, if your warp is threaded at 10 threads per inch, you should weave about 10 weft threads (or picks) per inch, or **ppi**. The projects indicate the number of weft threads per inch desired for the fabric.

- If 1 or more warp threads become loose after you have wound forward, and you cannot access the knots, insert a small piece of cardboard or a stick underneath them at the back beam.

- Measure your weaving as you go. Even though the instructions might say, "weave as long a piece as possible," it's nice to know how far you've gone. Use a safety pin or removable stitch marker to mark the edge. Measure and move the marker up before you advance your warp. Keep a note pad next to you for tracking your progress.

- To fix a broken warp thread, cut a new piece of yarn 12" longer than the remaining length of the warp. Thread it through the correct hole or slot. Insert a T-pin into the woven fabric as shown and wrap 1 tail around it. Tie the other tail onto a weight and hang it over the back beam without letting the weight hit the floor. As you wind forward, keep lowering the weight. When you have cut the piece off the loom, use a tapestry needle to weave in both tails along the warp, overlapping by at least 1".

- When your weaving is complete, weave in some waste yarn at the top edge and then remove the weaving from the loom. If you are planning to have fringe at either or both ends, untie the knots from the front apron rod and leave long warp tails. If you are planning to hem the piece, you can cut the fabric from the front apron rod.

- Lay the fabric out flat and, placing a tape measure along the center of the fabric, measure the length. Keep notes! (See Project Planner, page 19.)

- Machine stitch the raw edges. A zigzag stitch is best, but if you don't have this option, machine stitch a couple of rows of small, straight stitches. This stitching secures the weft until the edge is hemmed.

Before washing.

Hand washed gently, no agitation.

Machine washed, laid flat to dry.

Hand washed hot and cold, with agitation, and machine dried.

FINISHING THE FABRIC

HEMSTITCHING

If you are planning to leave short fringe, work hemstitching at the beginning and end while the weaving is still on the loom. After you weave in your heading, work hemstitching along the bottom edge as follows: Leaving a tail 3 times as long as the width of your fabric hanging off the right edge (or your dominant edge), weave 5–10 picks. Thread the tail through a blunt tapestry needle and bring the needle under the fabric, then up to the surface 4 warp threads over and 2 weft threads up. Pull yarn through. Bring the needle around the same 4 warp threads, forming a loop along the bottom edge of the fabric. Bring the needle to the surface of the fabric, pull the yarn through the loop, and tighten the knot; repeat across. Weave the tail into the last bundle of 4 warp threads.

hemstitching

1 Bring needle under fabric, then up to the surface 4 warp threads over and 2 weft threads up.

2 Pull yarn through. Bring needle around same 4 warp threads, forming a loop along bottom edge of fabric.

3 Bring needle to surface of fabric, pull yarn through loop.

4 Tighten knot; repeat across.

At the end of the weaving, leave a long tail of weft at your dominant side and work as above EXCEPT bring the needle through the fabric 4 warp threads over and 2 weft threads down.

TWISTED FRINGE

If leaving long fringe, you have a few choices. You can hemstitch as described above, or you can tie several threads together with an overhand knot. In either case, leave the fringe loose or twist each group as follows: Divide threads into 2 even sets. Holding 1 set in each hand, twist both sets in the same direction, then twist the sets together in the opposite direction. Tie an overhand knot at the bottom to hold the twist.

twisted fringe

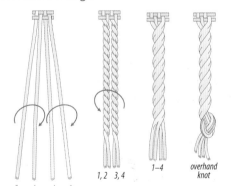

1   2   3   4

1,2 3,4

1–4

overhand knot

Twist each pair of strands separately to the right, then twist the 2 twisted pairs together to the left. Secure with an overhand knot.

WET FINISHING/WASHING

The next step is to wash your weaving. The process is called **fulling** and is a must for all woven fabrics destined to be clothing. It enhances the drape and feel, and is the finishing touch that transforms interwoven fibers into fabric. I generally hand wash fabrics I've woven for clothing.

FINISHING WOOL AND OTHER ANIMAL FIBERS

Fill the sink with tepid water and a no-rinse wool wash—enough to cover the woven fabric (no-rinse just makes it easier). Swish the fabric in the water, squeezing the cloth repeatedly. Unlike when washing knit fabric, you **want** to agitate so the fibers can bind together. Gently squeeze out the excess water—do not wring. Wrap in a towel or put through a short spin cycle in your washing machine. Lay flat on towels to dry.

For a tighter, more fulled or felt-like fabric, wash the weaving in the washing machine. Do it slowly, looking at it frequently, until you've achieved the desired effect. Washing in hot water and rinsing with cold will create the most fulling.

FINISHING COTTON AND OTHER PLANT MATERIALS

Hand wash in cool water with a few drops of dishwashing liquid. Rinse. Rinse again, adding a teaspoon of white vinegar—this will help remove any soap residue and will also bind any colors that might have run. Wrap in towels or run through the spin cycle in your washing machine. Put cotton in the dryer on low heat until just damp; then lay flat on a towel to dry. For all other plant materials, just lay flat on a towel to dry.

Techniques index

abbreviations

g gram(s)
" inch(es)
k knit(ting)(s)(ted)
m meter(s)
mm millimeter(s)
oz ounce(s)
p purl(ed)(ing)(s)
RS right side(s)
sc single crochet
WS wrong side(s)
yd(s) yard(s)

Knitting is a useful option for finishing edges and for creating garment pieces that would otherwise require a great deal of cutting and sewing. For the projects in this book, I've added knit sleeves, buttonbands, and collars, as well as gussets to widen a sleeve or add swing to a jacket. Knitting widens panels for a tote bag and makes the back of a man's vest. Ribbing forms the bands of woven hats. A knit lace border embellishes a blouse. Knit edges disguise un-seamly (pun intended) selvedges.

KNITTING TOOLS

- Knitting needles in an assortment of sizes (see suggestions for individual projects). I prefer circular needles, especially for picking up stitches along edges.

- A needle gauge is useful for checking the size of knitting needles.

- Crochet hooks in assorted sizes. A steel #1 or #2 crochet hook is helpful for picking up stitches through 2 layers of woven fabric.

- Tapestry needle

- Stitch markers — regular and removable

- Stitch holder

pick up & knit (PUK)

With RS facing and yarn in back, insert needle from front to back, 1 warp thread in from edge and through a return loop of weaving. Knit a stitch.

TIPS FOR PICKING UP STITCHES IN WOVEN FABRIC

- Always pick up stitches into a selvedge or hemmed edge, never along a raw or zigzagged edge.

- Knitting should be added to woven fabric only after the weaving has been washed and dried.

- Knit a gauge swatch with your yarn and the suggested needle size in the specified pattern stitch. Measure the stitches per inch. Pick up that number of stitches per inch.

- Use a smaller-sized needle to pick up stitches, then change to the needle used to achieve the required gauge.

- Always pick up and knit (PUK) from the RS of the fabric, unless otherwise directed.

- Use a crochet hook when you need to pick up stitches through 2 layers of fabric.

- A general rule is to [pick up a stitch, skip 2 warp threads or weft threads] across, as shown. If there is a stitch multiple for the pattern stitch OR the need exists to pick up a specific number of stitches, pick up stitches by the general rule, then increase or decrease stitches in the next row to get to the number required.

BASIC STITCHES TO USE WITH WEAVING

Choose knit stitches that will complement the weaving. To make the design even more cohesive, use one of the yarns from the woven fabric for the knitting. Here are some good, basic stitches that will work well with weaving:

Garter
Knit every row.

Stockinette
Knit RS rows; purl WS rows.

Reverse stockinette
Purl RS rows. Knit WS rows.

Seed
Row 1 (RS) [K1, p1] to end.
All other rows Purl the knit stitches and knit the purl stitches.

Half-linen
OVER AN ODD NUMBER OF STITCHES
Row 1 (RS) K1, [slip 1 with yarn in front (wyif), k1] to end. *Rows 2 and 4* Purl.
Row 3 K2, [slip 1 wyif, k1] to last stitch, k1.

Basketweave
MULTIPLE OF 4
Row 1 (RS) [K2, p2] to end.
Rows 2 and 4 Purl the purl stitches and knit the knit stitches.
Row 3 [P2, k2] to end.

3-needle bind-off

 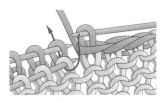

1 With stitches on 2 needles, place RS together. [Knit 2 stitches together (1 from front needle and 1 from back needle, as shown)] twice.

2 With left needle, pass first stitch on right needle over second stitch and off right needle.

3 Knit next 2 stitches together.

4 Repeat Steps 2 and 3, end by cutting yarn and drawing through the last stitch (see Fasten off, page 12).

3-NEEDLE BIND-OFF

If you have added knit panels to edges that need to be joined, binding the stitches off together is a nice alternative to sewing. It is usually done on the WS, but if worked on the RS, with the WS held together, it creates a decorative edge.

Work the panels as indicated in the pattern, leaving the stitches of the first panel on a spare needle. Work the second panel, then hold both pieces together and bind off as shown.

SINGLE CROCHET EDGING ON WOVEN FABRIC

With RS facing and yarn in back, insert a crochet hook from front to back into the selvedge or hemmed edge, 1 warp thread from edge and through a return loop of weaving (see Pick up & knit, page 10); single crochet. Space single crochets as needed to maintain a flat edge.

WET FINISHING

If knitting has been added, steam the knit areas. If the knitting needs to be blocked, pin the pieces to the desired shape on your ironing board. Wet a towel and lay it on top of the knitting. Hold a steam iron lightly on top of the towel and let the steam infuse the fabric, then allow it to dry before removing pins.

TECHNIQUES

knit cast-on

1 Start with a slip knot on left needle (first cast-on stitch). Insert right needle into slip knot from front. Wrap yarn over right needle as if to knit.

2 Bring yarn through slip knot, forming a loop on right needle.

3 Insert left needle under loop and slip loop off right needle. One additional stitch cast on.

4 Insert right needle into last stitch on left needle as if to knit. Knit a stitch and transfer it to the left needle as in Step 3. Repeat Step 4 for each additional stitch.

purl (p)

1 With yarn in front of work, insert right needle into stitch from back to front.

2 Bring yarn over right needle from front to back.

3 Bring yarn through stitch with right needle. Pull stitch off left needle. Repeat Steps 1–3.

knit (k)

1 With yarn in back of work, insert right needle into stitch on left needle from front to back.

2 Bring yarn between needles and over right needle.

3 Bring yarn through stitch with right needle. Pull stitch off left needle.

Knit stitch completed. Repeat Steps 1–3.

bind off

Knitwise

1 Knit 2 stitches.

2 With left needle, pass first stitch on right needle over second stitch (above) and off needle: 1 stitch bound off (next drawing).

3 Knit 1 more stitch.

4 Pass first stitch over second. Repeat Steps 3 and 4.
When last loop is on right needle, break yarn and pull tail of yarn through loop (see Fasten off).

Purlwise

Work Steps 1–4 of Bind-off Knitwise *EXCEPT* purl the stitches instead of knitting them.

fasten off

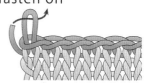

Work bind-off until only 1 stitch remains on right needle. Cut yarn and fasten off stitch as shown above.

chain stitch

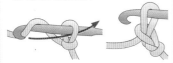

1 Make a slip knot to begin. **2** Catch yarn and draw through loop on hook (left). First chain made (right). Repeat Step 2.

single crochet (sc)

1 Insert hook into a stitch, catch yarn and pull up a loop. Catch yarn and pull through the loop on the hook.

2 Insert hook into next stitch to the left.

3 Catch yarn and pull through the stitch; 2 loops on hook.

4 Catch yarn and pull through both loops on hook; 1 single crochet completed. Repeat Steps 2–4.

knit into front & back (kf&b)

1 Knit into front of next stitch on left needle, but do not pull the stitch off needle.

2 Take right needle to back, then knit through the back of the same stitch.

3 Pull stitch off left needle. Completed increase: 2 stitches from 1 stitch. This increase results in a purl bump after the knit stitch.

SSK *A left-slanting single decrease*

1 Slip 2 stitches separately to right needle as if to knit.

2 Slip left needle into these 2 stitches from left to right and knit them together:

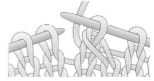

2 stitches become 1.

yarn over (yo)

Bring yarn under the needle to the front, take it over the needle to the back, and knit the next stitch.

slip purlwise (sl 1 p-wise)

1 Insert right needle into next stitch on left needle from back to front (as if to purl).

2 Slide stitch from left to right needle. Stitch orientation does not change (right leg of stitch loop is at front of needle).

The stitch slipped purlwise can be a knit or a purl.

slip knitwise (sl 1 k-wise)

1 Insert right needle into next stitch on left needle from front to back (as if to knit).

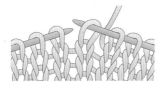

2 Slide stitch from left to right needle. Stitch orientation changes (right leg of stitch loop is at back of needle).

The stitch slipped knitwise can be a knit or a purl.

slip with yarn on RS of work (wyif, wyib)

Move the yarn to the front on a RS row …

… or to the back on a WS row before slipping a stitch. This places the yarn on the RS of the fabric.

k2tog *A right-slanting single decrease*

1 Insert right needle into first 2 stitches on left needle, beginning with second stitch from end of left needle.

2 Knit these 2 stitches together as if they were 1.

13

I am not a seamstress. In fact, I must confess, I have never sewn a garment from a sewing pattern. I am much more comfortable sewing by hand than by machine. Some of my sewing techniques may not be standard, but they work well with handwoven textiles. Many of the seams and all of the hems are hand sewn, either with yarn or with sewing thread. A sewing machine is useful for stitching the fabric before it is cut, in order to keep it from unraveling.

SEWING TOOLS

Use a **sewing machine** with zigzag capability, if possible. I have a small, inexpensive machine that allows me to choose various sizes of straight and zigzag stitches (a Singer Pixie Plus).

A **dress form** in your size is nice to have, though it is not absolutely necessary. I have one with removable arms so I can better see how a garment will drape. Dress the form in a skirt to help you visualize the total look.

SEWING TIPS

- Make a garment out of muslin before you think about weaving it—this will help you decide on sizing and design. Using fabric markers on the muslin will help you understand how the placement of stripes or other design elements will work within a shape.

- The structure of weaving provides vertical and horizontal lines to follow when you are sewing. If, because of color or texture, it is not easy to follow a horizontal line for cutting and sewing, use a T-square to ensure a straight, horizontal line. Mark the line, first with pins and then with chalk.

- Most of the projects in this book require that you weave a long piece of cloth and cut it into sections. To do this, machine stitch 2 lines—of zigzag if possible—about ½" apart from each other, then cut between them. Use a contrasting color of thread so the lines are visible.

I ALSO USE

- Fabric markers in a variety of colors
- Marking pencil or chalk
- Muslin
- Tru-Grid Pellon®
- Sewing needle and thread
- Sharp scissors
- Steam iron
- Straight pins with colored tips (easier to find in the rug)
- T-square

FINISHING THE GARMENT

If finishing requires overlapping 2 hems, 1 horizontal and 1 vertical, you can reduce the bulk by trimming away the corner of 1 of the hems.

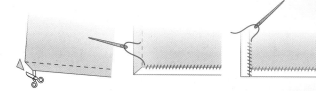

Another option is to cut off the corner of both hems. Fold up both hems, turning under the raw edges (including at the corner), then sew the hems by hand. Sew the miter closed.

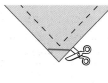 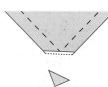 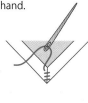

A SEAM FOR EVERY REASON

WORKING WITH RAW EDGES

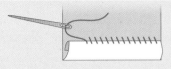

HEM Allow ¾–1" of woven fabric. Fold raw edge under and sew by hand with sewing thread. The hem blends in when turned to either the RS or the WS of the fabric.

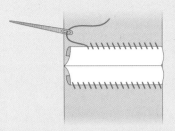

SEAM Machine or hand sew 2 raw edges together. Turn raw edges of seam allowance under and stitch by hand with sewing thread.

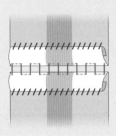

BLIND STITCH Hand sew 2 hemmed edges together using matching yarn. This is useful when aligning stripes.

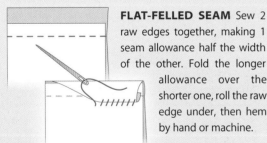

FLAT-FELLED SEAM Sew 2 raw edges together, making 1 seam allowance half the width of the other. Fold the longer allowance over the shorter one, roll the raw edge under, then hem by hand or machine.

WORKING WITH FINISHED EDGES

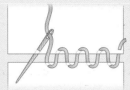

BASEBALL STITCH Worked with matching yarn for a flat, invisible seam.

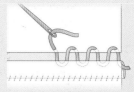

SEWING HEM TO SELVEDGE Use Blind Stitch for the rolled edge (lower edge) and Baseball Stitch for the selvedge (upper edge).

BACK STITCH For a raised, visible seam on the RS. Sew with matching yarn.

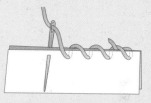

OVERHAND STITCH Work with matching yarn from the RS.

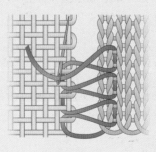

MATTRESS STITCH For sewing woven edge to woven edge or woven edge to knit edge. Stitch between first and second warp threads.

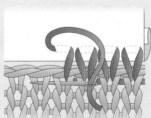

GRAFT HEMMED EDGE OF WOVEN FABRIC TO BOUND-OFF EDGE OF KNIT FABRIC Holding needle parallel to edge and alternating between edges, weave pieces together. Insert needle through hemmed edge of weaving, then through knit stitches just inside the bound-off edge.

GRAFT BOUND-OFF EDGES TOGETHER Align stitches as shown, graft over finished edges, and adjust tension.

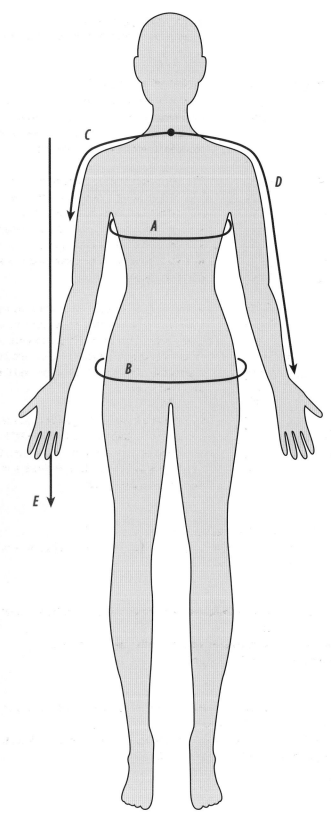

A Chest measurement _____
Measure around chest at widest point and add at least 4" for ease. Divide this number by 2 = width of back/front of garment.

B Hip measurement _____
Measure around hips and add at least 4" for ease. If garment is hip length or longer, use whichever measurement is larger — A or B — to determine garment width.

C Drop shoulder measurement _____
Measure from center back of neck to desired drop point on arm. Multiply by 2. Compare this measurement to chest and hip measurements while deciding on the best width for the garment.

D Sleeve length _____
Measure from center back of neck to wrist. Subtract half the width of the back = length of sleeve.

E Length of garment _____
Measure from top of shoulder at base of neck to desired length.

Measuring yourself or the person for whom you are making a garment is critical to creating a successful piece. Just as important is adding the correct number of inches to the body measurement to achieve the desired fit — this is called *ease*. I have suggested adding at least 4" of ease to the largest measurement, as these garments are designed to drape and not hug the body. If the garment requires, you might also need to add for seam allowances: add ¼–½" for each seam if they are finished edges, ¾–1" for raw edges.

TIP Plan for more width and length than you think you might want. Pieces can always be made narrower and shorter.

This book is about weaving projects that require minimal cutting and sewing. You are not weaving yardage, but rather the actual pattern pieces. Planning the shape and size of these pieces is the first step.

WIDTH OF PIECE

1 Start with the **desired finished width** of each piece.

Note that the back or front of a garment might be comprised of 2 or more pieces.

2 Add 1" for **draw-in** as you weave.

3 Add another 1" or more for **shrinkage** in washing.

Sampling will give you a more accurate idea of how much width you will need to add to reach your desired finished width.

The total is the **width in the heddle/reed.**

LENGTH OF PIECE

1 Decide on **desired finished length** of piece, hemmed.

2 Add an additional 2" for **hem allowances** at top and bottom edges.

3 Add 10–15% for **draw-up** and **shrinkage**.

Draw-up means that your piece will measure less when it relaxes off the loom than when it was measured under tension. It will also shrink with washing.

The total is the **weaving length** per woven piece**.**

CALCULATE WARP LENGTH

1 Add the **weaving lengths** of all pieces together.

2 Add 24–36" (depending on your loom) for **loom waste.**

The total is the **warp length.**

USING THE PROJECT PLANNER
Copy the Project Planner on page 19 and fill in the numbers.

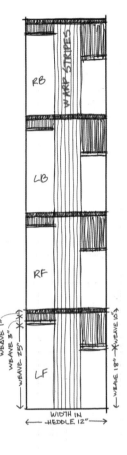

PLAN YOUR WARP

Draw a diagram showing all of the pieces together on the warp. Indicate the width in the heddle and the length you need to weave for each piece. This is called a *schematic*; we have provided schematics for each project.

All of the pieces that are the same width can be woven on the same warp. For most of the projects in this book, the woven pieces are rectangles; the pieces are woven on a continuous warp and the fabric is cut into separate pieces. Weave as long a piece as possible, measuring as you go. Note as **length of weaving measured on the loom** (under tension) on the Project Planner on page 19.

On my rigid-heddle loom, I plan warps that are no longer than 4 yards. One reason is that this is the maximum distance I have between the warping peg clamped to my dining room table and the end of the room. Another is that, with some heavier yarns, the fabric would become too thick around the cloth beam if the warp were longer.

If your loom allows for a longer warp, you can combine several warps into one. Note that this saves the 24" loom waste for each additional warp. If some pieces are narrower than others, weave the wider ones first and then eliminate some warp threads to weave the narrower pieces.

CALCULATE YARN REQUIREMENTS

Once you have determined the width and length of your warp (or warps), you can calculate how much yarn you will need.

WARP

1 Multiply the **width in the heddle/reed** × sett (warp threads per inch) = total **number of warp threads**.

2 Multiply **number of warp threads** × **warp length** = length in inches.

3 Divide length in inches by 36 = length in yards.

WEFT

1 Multiply estimated **picks per inch** (ppi) × **weaving length** (not including loom waste) = total **number of picks** to weave.

2 Multiply total **number of picks** × **width in the heddle/reed** = length in inches.

3 Divide length in inches by 36 = length in yards.

SPECIAL CONSIDERATIONS FOR SHAPING ON THE LOOM

In order to conserve as many finished edges as possible, I shape armholes and necklines on the loom rather than cutting into the fabric. When planning your pattern pieces, draw the armhole and neckline shapes and indicate the measurements you need to weave. Remember to consider width and length shrinkage. If you want a finished armhole measurement of 9", for example, you need to weave 10".

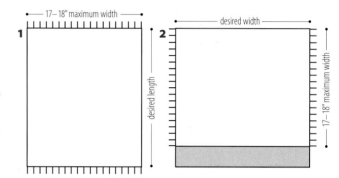

▨ Hem   ▨ Waste yarn

THE SLEEVE CHALLENGE

The top of the sleeve has to be wide enough to fit into the armhole. The finished sleeve width, after washing and seaming, might need to be 22"—not possible with a 20" loom (**1**).

A FEW DESIGN OPTIONS

CHANGE THE PLAN

Use the length of the fabric to achieve the desired width (**2**). In this case, the sleeve might only be 17–18" long—the finished width of your fabric if using a 20" loom. Add to the length with either a knit cuff (*Light & Shade Jacket*) or by attaching another woven panel (*Be Bold Jacket*).

KNIT THE SLEEVE

The entire sleeve can be knit (*Mad Plaid Jacket, Summer Dress Whites*).

KNIT GUSSETS

Pick up stitches along the side edges of a woven panel and knit to the desired width (**3**). By working short rows, you can create a sleeve that tapers at the wrist (*Light & Shade Jacket*).

Another solution is a knit insert (**4**) down the center of the sleeve (*Big Pocket Jacket*).

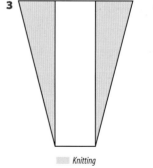
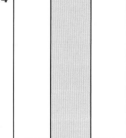

▨ Knitting

SHAPE CUFFS

Sometimes a straight, rectangular sleeve works well (*Sorbet Jacket*); but other times you want it to cinch in at the wrist. Consider a pinch or a pleat to create the look you want (*Big Pockets Jacket* and *Be Bold Jacket*).

PLAY WITH PATTERNS

Because the sleeves are usually wider than the width of the panels woven for the body, a separate warp is required. This opens up the possibility of designing a coordinating but different pattern for these pieces (*Sorbet Jacket, Be Bold Jacket*).

PROJECT PLANNER

NAME OF PROJECT_____

YARNS: Name, color, fiber content   WGT/YDS

A _____   _____

B _____   _____

C _____   _____

D _____   _____

E _____   _____

SETT (warp threads per inch)   _____

WARP LENGTH

Desired finished length, hemmed   _____

Add at least 2" for **hem allowance**   +_____

Add 10–15% for **draw-up** and **shrinkage**   +_____

Weaving length   =_____

Add at least 24" for **loom waste**   +_____

Total warp length   =_____

Length of weaving measured on the loom (under tension)   _____

Length of weaving measured off the loom (relaxed)   _____

Length of finished fabric (after washing)   _____

WARP WIDTH

Desired finished width   _____

Add at least 2" for **draw-in** and **shrinkage**   + 2"

Total **width in the heddle/reed**   =_____

Width on the loom (after draw-in)   _____

Width of finished fabric (after washing)   _____

NUMBER OF WARP THREADS

Width in the heddle/reed × **sett**

Total **number of warp threads**   =_____

WARP ORDER

WEFT ORDER

_____

_____

_____

_____

YARDAGE REQUIRED FOR WARP

Count threads per yarn/color

____ A threads × warp length _____ = ____ yds color A

____ B threads × warp length _____ = ____ yds color B

____ C threads × warp length _____ = ____ yds color C

____ D threads × warp length _____ = ____ yds color D

____ E threads × warp length _____ = ____ yds color E

____ Total threads (should match calculated **number of warp threads**)

YARDAGE REQUIRED FOR WEFT (estimate)

Estimated **picks per inch** (ppi) ____

Total **weaving length** ____ × ppi ____ = total **number of picks** ____

Total number of picks ____ × warp width _____" = _____" ÷ 36 = _____ yds

Divide by number of colors for average yardage required per color _____ yds

WEFT	WARP + WEFT
A ____ yds	A ____ yds
B ____ yds	B ____ yds
C ____ yds	C ____ yds
D ____ yds	D ____ yds
E ____ yds	E ____ yds

Keeping records of your projects is a good habit to develop. Complete the on-the loom, off-the-loom, and finished fabric measurements.
Include labels and windings from your yarn and a photo or swatch of your weaving. Keep it all in a plastic sleeve for future reference.

This is my favorite part. I get to play with my yarns, looking at them in different combinations. How do I mix them? What will look good together and on me? I've organized my stash by color — a warm drawer with reds, oranges, and yellows; a cool drawer with blues, purples, and teals; a drawer of neutrals; etc. I like seeing the different textures and shades in each color family.

There are various ways to work with color, and there are volumes written on the subject. I will tell you about some of the ways I think about color and will give you some ideas about how to design your weaving.

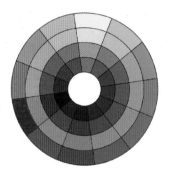

CHOOSING COLORS

● Pull out lots of colors that you think will work together — more than you will actually use. Next, go through a process of elimination. Does this color add or detract from the color scheme? Narrow it down. Squint at the collection. Is it missing something? Try adding a complementary color from the opposite side of the color wheel. If using red, try green; if using blue, try orange.

● Stuck in a color rut? Look at a photo, painting, or textile that attracts you and then, from your stash, pull all of the colors you can identify.

● Nature is a great color resource: Look at water patterns, trees in the forest, sunsets, rocks, flowers ....

DESIGNING WITH COLOR

Color wraps are a way to help you visualize how colors will play together.

Here's a good exercise: Collect all of the colors from a photograph you like. Cut a piece of cardboard 2 × 8" and do a wrapping. Think about proportions: Is there just a splash of red in the photo? Then wrap just a splash of red yarn. What colors surround it in the photo? Match that in your wrapping.

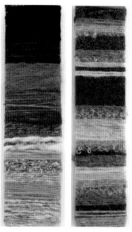

Another design technique I sometimes use is to work with water-soluble colored pencils or crayons. For the Aegean Tunic (page 54), my process started with a group of yarns that I wanted to use.

First, I did little paintings with matching water-soluble crayons.

Next, I did a color wrapping.

Finally, to plan the warp stripes, I used a knitters' design program to create a graph on the computer. Or, you could use graph paper and colored pencils.

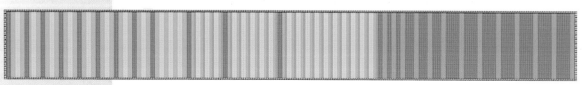

DESIGNING WARPS AND THREADING THE LOOM

All of the fabrics in this book are woven in plain weave, using a rigid-heddle loom or 2 shafts. The Warp Order (also called a draft) provides you with the information you need to warp your loom for the fabric shown. The bottom row represents slot threads or threads on Shaft 1. The top row represents hole threads or threads on Shaft 2. Read the drafts from right to left (if you are left-handed and threading your loom from left to right, read the drafts from left to right and make Row 1 the holes and Row 2 the slots).

A striped warp in colors A and B

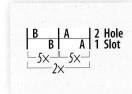

This draft tells you to wind 10 warp threads of A. To accomplish this on a rigid-heddle loom, tie A onto the back apron rod, [pull a loop through a slot] 5 times; this creates 10 warp threads. Cut and tie A to the back rod. Tie B onto the back rod and repeat. Repeat the whole sequence once more — 40 warp threads.

Alternate 2 threads of A with 2 threads of B

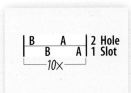

Since, with Direct Warping, you are pulling a loop through a slot, you automatically get 2 threads of the same color next to each other. To alternate colors, start by tying both colors to the back apron rod, then [pull a loop of A through the first slot, then a loop of B through the next slot; you now have 2 threads of A followed by 2 threads of B] 10 times — 40 warp threads.

A 2-color log cabin pattern

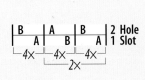

The colors alternate as follows: [(1A, 1B) 4 times for 8 warp threads, then (1B, 1A) 4 times for 8 warp threads] twice (for a total of 32 warp threads), then end with [1A, 1B] 4 times — 8 warp threads; for a total of 40 warp threads.

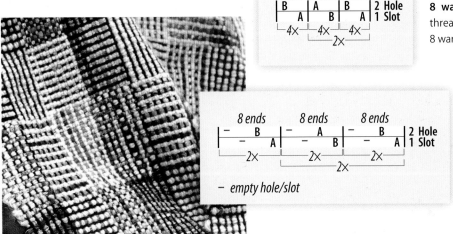

Möbius Cowl on page 110 is a 3-color log cabin pattern.

− empty hole/slot

1 Warp 1 slot and 1 hole, then skip 1 slot and 1 hole.

2 Cut loops, then thread for Warp Order.

1 Since the colors alternate 1/1 instead of 2/2 in the log cabin pattern, follow the heddle illustration described below for the Direct Warping method:

*[Pull a loop of A through slot, pull a loop of B through the hole to the left of that slot; skip the next slot and hole] twice — 8 warp threads.

[Pull a loop of B through next slot, pull a loop of A through next hole; skip next slot and hole] twice — 8 warp threads; for a total of 16 warp threads. Repeat from * once more — 32 warp threads.

[Pull a loop of A through next slot, pull a loop of B through next hole; skip next slot and hole] twice — 8 warp threads; for a total of 40 warp threads.

2 After winding onto the back beam, cut the loops. [Pull 1 thread of A from the first slot and bring it through the empty slot next to it; pull 1 thread of B from the hole and bring it through the empty hole next to it] across; note that, in the first section, all of the A threads are in slots and the B threads are in holes. In the next section, the B threads are in slots and the A threads are in holes. By weaving in the same order, you can achieve some very interesting patterns.

DESIGNING WEFTS: TAKING THE PLAIN OUT OF PLAIN WEAVE

The weft can include as many colors and textures as you wish. If you weave with just 1 color in the weft, color changes in the warp will provide the main color interest. Alternating colors in the weft creates an interplay of warp and weft colors. To alternate colors, follow these steps:

1 Wind a shuttle for each color, A and B.

2 Weave A from right to left; bring the tail around the last warp thread and back into the same shed. Beat and change sheds.

3 Weave B from right to left; bring the tail around the last warp thread and back into the same shed. Beat and change sheds.

4 Both shuttles are now on the left. Look at the first warp thread on the left. If it is up, bring color A **over** color B and into the shed. If it is down, bring color A **under** color B and into the shed. Beat and change sheds.

5 Weave color B.

6 Now both shuttles are on the right. Look at the first warp thread on the right and follow the directions in Step 4.

This is your mantra: Up, over. Down, under. This will ensure that you catch the last warp thread when alternating colors.

If you've set up stripes in the warp and you weave stripes in the weft, you create a check or plaid pattern. I have mostly avoided horizontal stripes in my clothing. One reason is that it is difficult, even with careful counting and measuring, to match stripe patterns when sewing pieces together. In addition, vertical lines are more flattering to the figure than horizontal lines.

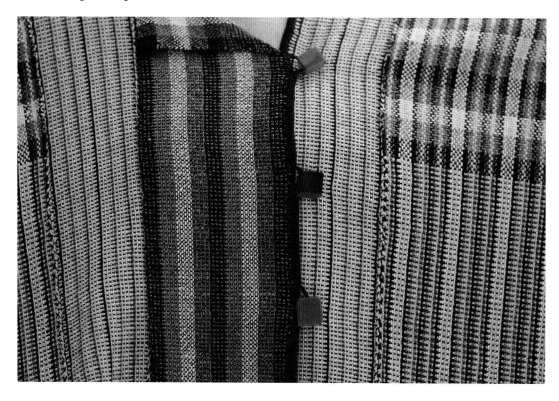

The yarns used for clothing should drape well and, ideally, resist pilling and shedding. Warp yarns need to be strong enough to withstand abrasion during weaving. Pull on the yarn firmly. If it drifts apart, it is not strong enough for warp; if it breaks with a snap, it's probably fine. Think silk, rayon, tencel, some cottons, bamboo, or merino wool. Avoid yarns with a lot of fluff, like mohair, especially for the warp. The warp threads will stick together and cause mistakes in your weaving.

If you are using the same yarns I used for a project, all of the decisions and calculations have been made for you. If you are substituting yarns, however, you will need to determine the sett (how many warp threads you will have per inch). The generally accepted standard for "good cloth" for clothing is a balanced weave or a slightly warp-faced cloth. A balanced weave has about the same number of weft picks per inch (ppi) as warp ends (or threads) per inch (epi). A slightly warp-faced fabric will have more epi than ppi. This sett allows for a fabric with good density as well as a nice drape.

This chart suggests which heddle to use with different weights of knitting yarns. Remember, it's just a general guideline. For instance, a smooth, silky, worsted-weight yarn might work better at 10 dpi than at 8 dpi.

Yarn weight	Knit stitches per inch	Wraps per inch	Dents per inch
5 Chunky	3–3.5	10–14	5
4 Worsted or aran	4–4.5	16–18	7.5/8
3 DK, light worsted, or doubled fingering	5–5.5	18–20	10
2 Sport or doubled lace	6–6.5	22–24	12/12.5

The way to determine the best sett for your yarn is to wrap the yarn around a ruler for 1", laying the wraps as closely together as possible without overlapping them. Count the wraps and divide by 2 — the answer is the sett. Choose the heddle that best matches. If in doubt, round up; it is always better to have a more closely sett warp. A loose warp allows for the weft to pack down more tightly — a fabric with less drape.

I often combine a heavier knitting yarn with a thin, lace-weight weaving yarn. This serves a dual purpose. First, I can obtain a lighter, more fluid fabric. Second, I use fewer yards of the more expensive knitting yarn.

One of the great pleasures of weaving is the ability to combine different fibers and textures. I generally use the same yarns for the warp as I do for the weft. And if I am adding knitting, I like to use the knitting yarn in the weaving as well, so choosing at least 1 yarn that will knit up nicely becomes an important consideration.

SAMPLING

In the end, the best way to know how your yarn choices will work is to sample. There are times I have sampled a piece at 10 dpi and had to change it to 12 dpi. Sometimes the colors I've chosen just didn't play as well together as I had imagined. Better to find out on a small piece than to waste yarn on a larger one.

Sampling on a rigid-heddle loom is fast and easy, with less waste than on a floor loom. Set up about a 5" wide, 30" long warp. After weaving an inch, if you don't like the sett, untie the warp from the front, slide the heddle off, and re-thread the warp through a different one. Weave the sample, trying different weft patterns. Remove from the loom and wash. If you are going to add knitting to your project, you can experiment here with different stitches.

If you are sure about your warp choice but not so clear about how you want to weave it, put on some extra warp to play with so you can experiment with weft choices before you start the actual woven piece.

MY PERSONAL DESIGN CHALLENGE:

To weave a summer shirt to go with my new pants, based on the Tweedy Shirt concept (page 62) and using yarn from my stash.

To help me visualize how the woven fabric would look with my pants, I drew a figure wearing the top and the pants, scanned the drawing, and printed out several copies.

Design idea 1

I tried being bold, but I was concerned that I wouldn't be able to get the horizontal lines in the fabric to line up.

Design idea 2

Next I thought about a simple vertical stripe with black, stenciled shapes, to mimic the design of the pants. My next step would be to create the stencil and test it on commercial fabric — this would tell me if the proportion of the stencil shapes was correct.

Design Idea 3

Then I thought about simple, bold, vertical stripes.

Design Idea 4

The winning idea was a fabric with interesting texture and free-form hatching lines. I thought I would like it better with the pants, AND the horizontal lines wouldn't have to match. Ironically, even without trying, a lot of the lines did line up, and I had to adjust the pieces when I put the garment together so that they wouldn't.

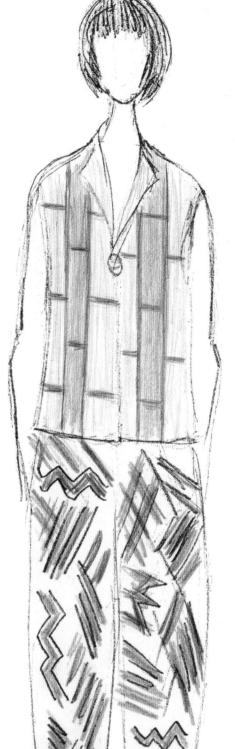

Tapestry technique allows you to *paint* with yarn, to create any shape in your textile that you can draw on paper. If you are working with plain weave on a rigid-heddle loom, tapestry opens up a whole new world of design possibilities. Introduce a small section of tapestry…

… or create an entire painting.

Tapestry usually refers to a weft-faced plain weave (the warp doesn't show), with patterning created by discontinuous wefts. The weft is usually beaten down very firmly to cover the warp. For this reason, contemporary tapestry weavers often use plied cottons or linens as warp, to endure the heavy beating.

If tapestry techniques are used but the warp is allowed to show, the fabric will be softer with more drape, suitable for clothing.

To achieve softness and drape, it is best to aim for a balanced weave. For example, if the warp is sett at 12 threads to the inch, then you should have about 12 weft threads per inch as well. Because the warp shows, the colors in the warp will interact with the weft. For a "blank canvas," use 1 color in the warp. For additional interest, plan a warp with stripes.

HATCHING
One of the simplest tapestry techniques is called hatching or, as the French say, hatchure. It was used in medieval tapestries for shading purposes. For clothing fabrics, hatching is a lovely way to introduce and blend colors.

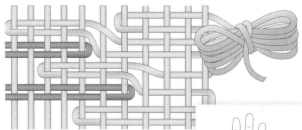

Weave color A from right to left and bring the shuttle out somewhere in the middle of the warp. Beat, change the shed, and return the shuttle to the right selvedge. Change the shed again, and weave color B from left to right, overlapping color A by 2 or more warp threads. Change the shed and return the shuttle to the left selvedge. Continue alternating colors, overlapping by as many warp threads as desired. If you find a small "hill" developing, fill in the depression by weaving an extra 2 rows in the same color.

You can use short stick shuttles but, for small amounts of a color, a bobbin (such as those used by knitters) or a **butterfly** made on your hand is useful.

Wrap yarn in figure-8 fashion around fingers. When finished, free fingers and wrap the last few inches around the center, then secure end.

weave • knit • wear

Following are diagrams showing joins for vertical, diagonal, and curved lines. (This is not meant to be a comprehensive course on tapestry techniques. There are several other joins, and people study tapestry for years to become proficient in using them. However, with what you learn here, you will be able to create the designs shown in this book and then proceed further on your own.)

Vertical line / Dovetail join

1 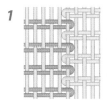 *THE COLORS OVERLAP BY 1 WARP.* Weave color A from left to right, bringing the shuttle out where you want the vertical line. Beat, change the shed and return shuttle to left edge. Change shed again and weave color B from right to left, bringing the shuttle out at the left of the shared warp thread. Change the shed and return to right edge around the shared warp thread. This works best when both yarns are the same weight.

Vertical line / Slit

2 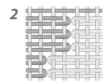 *THE COLORS MEET AT ADJOINING WARP THREADS AND DO NOT INTERLOCK, WHICH CREATES A SLIT.* Be careful not to pull the weft too tightly around the warp threads so they remain straight and don't create a large hole. If you are working with yarns of different weights, work more rows of the thinner yarn to maintain equal height on either side of the slit.

Diagonal line

3 *THE COLORS MEET AT ADJOINING WARP THREADS WITHOUT INTERLOCKING.* To prevent visible slits, the colors must move over by at least 1 warp thread for each turn. For a sharper angle, create steps as in **2**, and either leave slits or dovetail the colors together as in **1**.

Curved line

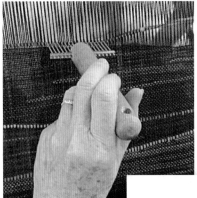

Start by building up the bottom shape, decreasing the number of warp threads used by at least 1 for each turn (**a**). When you have the desired shape, weave 1 or 2 picks of the same or contrasting color across the entire width (**b**) and use a fork or tapestry beater to beat the yarn down around the shape. Start filling in the overlapping shape (**c**). Remember to change the shed for each row and to increase the number of warp threads worked by at least 1. As soon as you have finished the motif, and the wefts form an even horizontal line, resume weaving across the entire warp, using the heddle to beat down the rows.

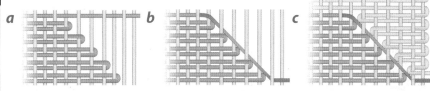

Woven with a 10-dent heddle in Manos del Uruguay Silk Blend.

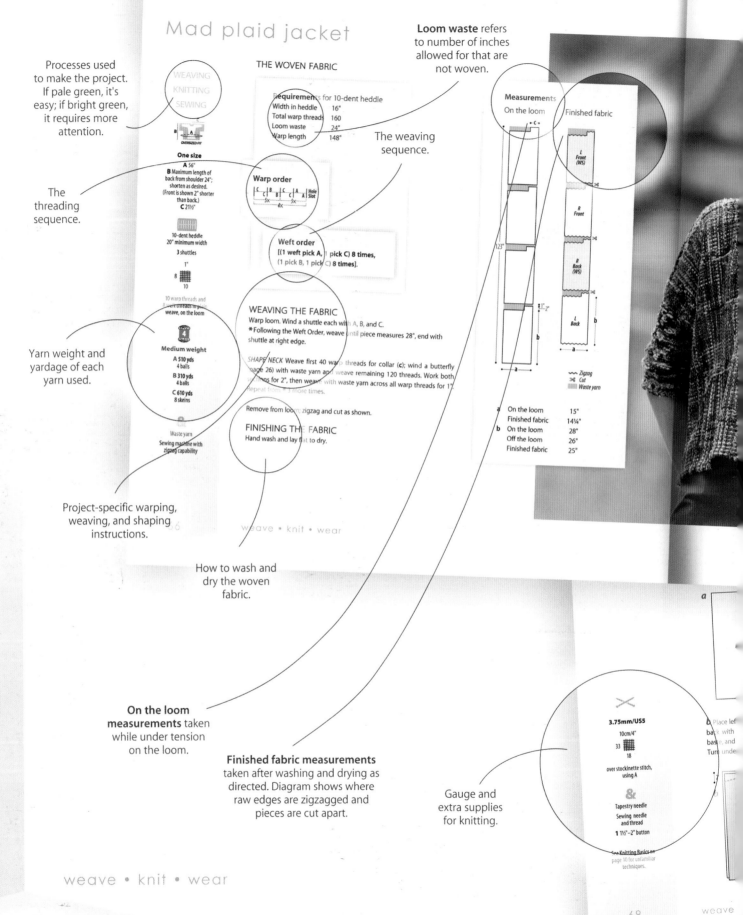

Mad plaid jacket

Processes used to make the project. If pale green, it's easy; if bright green, it requires more attention.

The threading sequence.

Yarn weight and yardage of each yarn used.

Project-specific warping, weaving, and shaping instructions.

How to wash and dry the woven fabric.

On the loom measurements taken while under tension on the loom.

Finished fabric measurements taken after washing and drying as directed. Diagram shows where raw edges are zigzagged and pieces are cut apart.

Gauge and extra supplies for knitting.

Loom waste refers to number of inches allowed for that are not woven.

The weaving sequence.

THE WOVEN FABRIC

Requirements for 10-dent heddle

Width in heddle	16"
Total warp threads	160
Loom waste	24"
Warp length	148"

Warp order

Weft order
[(1 weft pick A, 1 pick C) 8 times,
(1 pick B, 1 pick C) 8 times].

WEAVING THE FABRIC
Warp loom. Wind a shuttle each with A, B, and C.
*Following the Weft Order, weave until piece measures 28", end with shuttle at right edge.

SHAPE NECK Weave first 40 warp threads for collar (c); wind a butterfly (page 26) with waste yarn and weave remaining 120 threads. Work both sections for 2", then weave with waste yarn across all warp threads for 1". Repeat from * 3 more times.

Remove from loom; zigzag and cut as shown.

FINISHING THE FABRIC
Hand wash and lay flat to dry.

One size
A 56"
B Maximum length of back from shoulder 24"; shorten as desired. (Front is shown 2" shorter than back.)
C 21½"

10-dent heddle
20" minimum width

3 shuttles

1"

8 | 10

10 warp threads and 8 weft threads in plain weave, on the loom

Medium weight
A 510 yds 4 balls
B 310 yds 4 balls
C 610 yds 8 skeins

Waste yarn

Sewing machine with zigzag capability

Measurements
On the loom | Finished fabric

L Front (WS)

R Front

R Back (WS)

L Back

123"

1"–2"

~ Zigzag
✂ Cut
▓ Waste yarn

a	On the loom	15"
	Finished fabric	14¼"
b	On the loom	28"
	Off the loom	26"
	Finished fabric	25"

3.75mm/US5

10cm/4"

33 | 18

over stockinette stitch, using A

&

Tapestry needle
Sewing needle and thread
1 1½"–2" button

See Knitting Basics on page 10 for unfamiliar techniques.

OVERSIZED FIT

weave • knit • wear

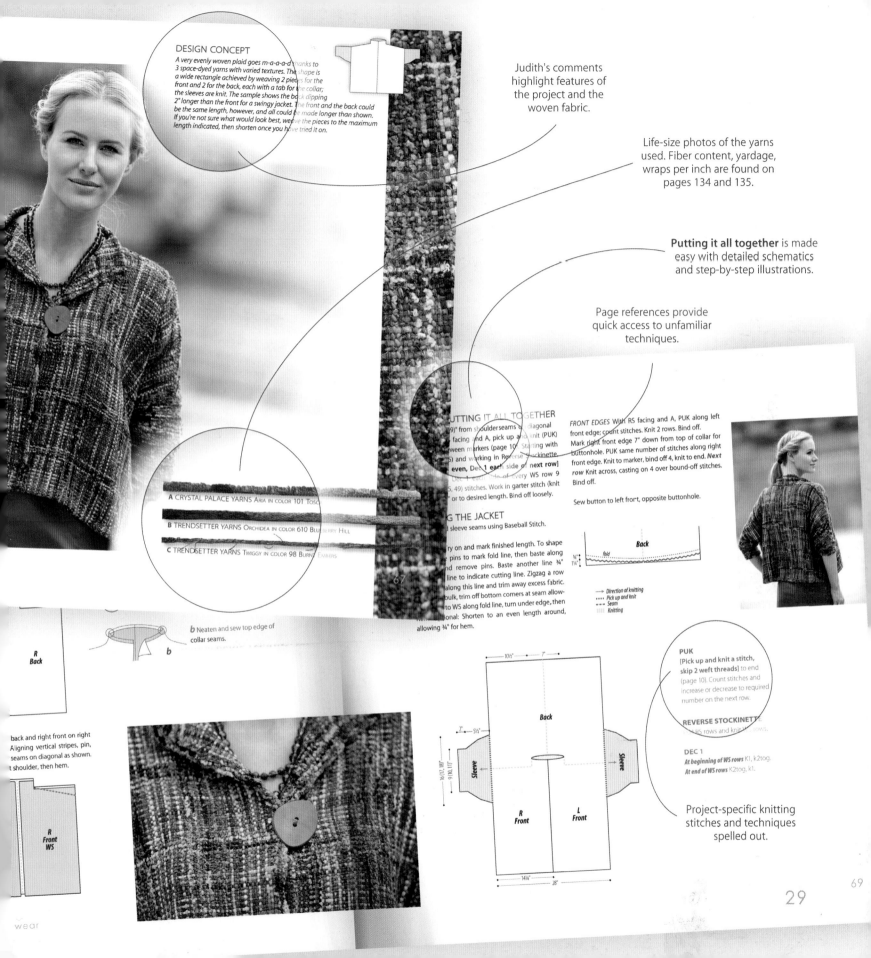

DESIGN CONCEPT

A very evenly woven plaid goes m-a-a-ad thanks to 3 space-dyed yarns with varied textures. The shape is a wide rectangle achieved by weaving 2 pieces for the front and 2 for the back, each with a tab for the collar; the sleeves are knit. The sample shows the back dipping 2" longer than the front for a swingy jacket. The front and the back could be the same length, however, and all could be made longer than shown. If you're not sure what would look best, weave the pieces to the maximum length indicated, then shorten once you have tried it on.

Judith's comments highlight features of the project and the woven fabric.

Life-size photos of the yarns used. Fiber content, yardage, wraps per inch are found on pages 134 and 135.

Putting it all together is made easy with detailed schematics and step-by-step illustrations.

Page references provide quick access to unfamiliar techniques.

A CRYSTAL PALACE YARNS ARIA in color 101 Tosca

B TRENDSETTER YARNS ORCHIDEA in color 610 BLUEBERRY HILL

C TRENDSETTER YARNS TWIGGY in color 98 BURNT EMBERS

PUTTING IT ALL TOGETHER

9)" from shoulder seams and diagonal facing and A, pick up and knit (PUK) ween markers (page 10). Starting with S) and working in Reverse Stockinette, **even, Dec 1 each side of next row]** Dec 1 each side of every WS row 9 5, 49) stitches. Work in garter stitch (knit or to desired length. Bind off loosely.

G THE JACKET

d sleeve seams using Baseball Stitch.

ry on and mark finished length. To shape pins to mark fold line, then baste along nd remove pins. Baste another line ¾" line to indicate cutting line. Zigzag a row along this line and trim away excess fabric. bulk, trim off bottom corners at seam allow-to WS along fold line, turn under edge, then ional: Shorten to an even length around, allowing ¾" for hem.

FRONT EDGES With RS facing and A, PUK along left front edge; count stitches. Knit 2 rows. Bind off. Mark right front edge 7" down from top of collar for buttonhole. PUK same number of stitches along right front edge. Knit to marker, bind off 4, knit to end. *Next row* Knit across, casting on 4 over bound-off stitches. Bind off.

Sew button to left front, opposite buttonhole.

Back

→ *Direction of knitting*
···· *Pick up and knit*
— *Seam*
▒ *Knitting*

b Neaten and sew top edge of collar seams.

b

R Back

back and right front on right Aligning vertical stripes, pin, seams on diagonal as shown. t shoulder, then hem.

R Front WS

PUK
[Pick up and knit a stitch, skip 2 weft threads] to end (page 10). Count stitches and increase or decrease to required number on the next row.

REVERSE STOCKINETTE
WS rows and knit WS rows.

DEC 1
At beginning of WS rows K1, k2tog.
At end of WS rows K2tog, k1.

Project-specific knitting stitches and techniques spelled out.

Back

Sleeve

Sleeve

R Front

L Front

10½"   7"

7" 5½"

16 (17, 18)"
9 (10, 11)"

14¼"
28"

Moderne serape

One size

55" × 20½",
including fringe

12- OR 12.5-dent heddle
20" minimum width

5 shuttles

1"

8
12 OR **12.5**

12 OR 12.5 warp threads
and 8 weft threads in plain
weave, on the loom

Medium weight

MC 1440 yds
7 skeins

A 90 yds
2 skeins

B 80 yds
1 skein

C 80 yds
1 skein

D 85 yds
1 skein

&

Safety pin

THE WOVEN FABRIC

Requirements for **12-** OR 12.5-dent heddle

Width in heddle	20"
Total warp threads	**240/250**
Loom waste	28"
Warp length	144"

Warp order

MC
MC
Hole
Slot

120/125 ×

Weft order

The technique used to create this pattern is called Discontinuous Weft — a tapestry technique that allows the warp to show. Two colors meet in the middle and return around the same warp thread to connect them (see Dovetail Join, page 27).

WEAVING THE FABRIC

Wind a shuttle each with A, B, C, and D. Wind a shuttle with MC. Warp loom and weave heading. Weave 5 weft picks of MC. Work 1 row of Hemstitch (page 9).

Open the next shed and locate a central warp thread in the down position. Mark with a safety pin or clip that is easily removable. Following Stripe Chart for colors, work Dovetail Join (page 27) as follows: *With A, start at left edge and weave across, bringing up shuttle in same space as marked warp thread. With D, start at right edge and bring up shuttle in same space. Change shed. The marked warp thread is now in the up position. Bring A around it from right to left and through the shed to the left edge. Bring D around it from left to right and through the shed to the right edge. Beat and change shed.* Repeat from* to* once more. Weave 4 picks MC. Carrying A and D along edges, work another 4-row stripe. Cut colors A and D and weave in ends. Carry MC along side edge and weave 4 picks. Continue to work colors as shown on chart, moving the marker frequently. The colors always meet and return around this same warp thread.

Work a total of 7 repeats of Stripe Chart, then work Rows 1–12 again. Work 5 picks of MC; end with 1 row of Hemstitch.

Weave 4" waste, then weave another piece, starting and ending with hemstitching. Remove from loom, leaving warp fringe at top and bottom edges to be trimmed later. Cut pieces apart, removing waste and leaving warp fringe at cut edges.

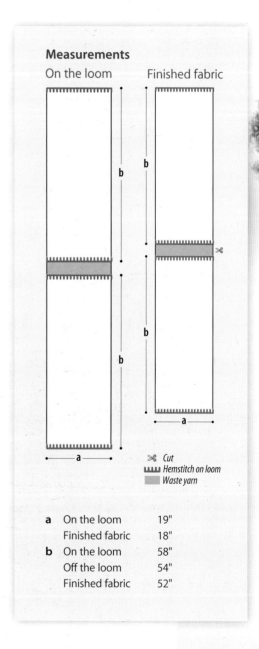

Measurements

On the loom   Finished fabric

b

b

b

b

b

a   a

✂ *Cut*
⊔⊔⊔⊔ *Hemstitch on loom*
▓▓▓ *Waste yarn*

a	On the loom	19"
	Finished fabric	18"
b	On the loom	58"
	Off the loom	54"
	Finished fabric	52"

FINISHING THE FABRIC

Hand wash. Wrap in towels or use spin cycle to remove excess water. Lay flat on towels to dry.

DESIGN CONCEPT

Two rectangles are joined with knitting for a contemporary serape that you can wear two ways. Hemstitching on the loom allows for short fringe, and the knit edges add a nice finishing touch.

Stripe chart

			Rows 61–64
C		B	Rows 57–60
			Rows 53–56
C		B	Rows 49–52
			Rows 45–48
D		A	Rows 41–44
			Rows 37–40
D		A	Rows 33–36
			Rows 29–32
B		C	Rows 25–28
			Rows 21–24
B		C	Rows 17–20
			Rows 13–16
A		D	Rows 9–12
			Rows 5–8
A		D	Rows 1–4

center warp

Legend:
- MC
- A
- B
- C
- D

MC CASCADE YARNS Pure Alpaca in color 3001 Black

TRENDSETTER YARNS Zoe in color

A 84 Carnation

TRENDSETTER YARNS Twiggy in colors

B 112 Smoke & Ash   **C** 92 Mushroom Soup

D PRISM YARNS Bon Bon in color 102

KNITTING THE BORDERS

Lay out both pieces as shown in diagram. Stripe colors should match at the top (shoulder) edges. Find the center of each top edge and place markers 5" from either side of center for neck edge. Place markers 4" from hemstitched edges. With RS facing and MC, pick up and knit (PUK) between markers *a* and *b* of Piece 1 (page 10). Knit 5 rows; leave stitches on needle. With another needle, PUK same number of stitches between markers *b* and *a* of Piece 2 and work to match. With WS together, work 3-Needle Bind-Off (page 11). Repeat between markers *d* and *c* of Piece 1 and between markers *c* and *d* of Piece 2.

With RS facing and MC, PUK along bottom edge of Piece 1. Knit 2 rows. Bind off. Repeat along bottom edge of Piece 2.

NECK EDGE With RS facing, MC, and beginning at shoulder seam, PUK around neck edge. Place marker and join to work in the round. Purl 1 round. Knit 1 round. Bind off in purl.

TOP EDGE SLITS With RS facing and MC, PUK along open top edges of Pieces 1 and 2. Knit 1 row. Bind off.

FINISHING THE SERAPE

Trim fringe to 1½". Steam press.

4.5mm/US7, 60cm (24") long AND spare needle for 3-Needle Bind-Off

10cm/4"

40

21

over garter stitch

&

Tapestry needle 8 removable stitch markers

See Knitting Basics on page 10 for unfamiliar techniques.

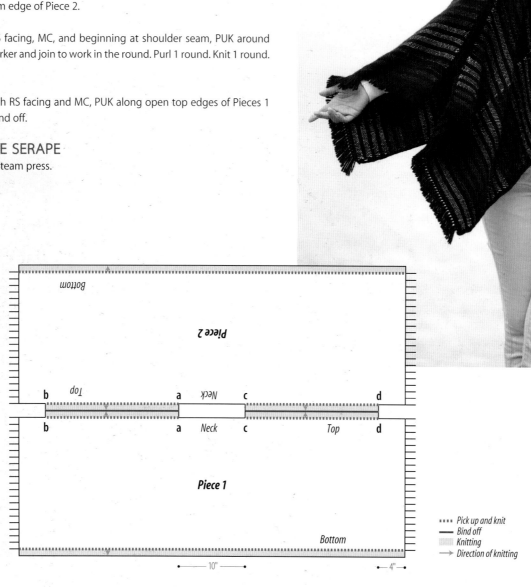

Pick up and knit
Bind off
Knitting
Direction of knitting

PUK
[Pick up and knit a stitch,
skip 2 weft threads]
to end (page 10).

Bark cloth ruana

S (M, L)

Shown in LARGE, page 37

35½ (40½, 45)" wide ×
26" long; shorten as desired

10-dent heddle
20" minimum width

6 shuttles

1"

11

10

10 warp threads and
11 weft threads in plain
weave, on the loom

Light weight

A 510 (560, 610) yds
5 skeins

Medium weight

B 250 (280, 300) yds
3 skeins

C 190 (210, 230) yds
2 (3, 3) skeins

D 220 (240, 260) yds
3 skeins

E 320 (360, 390) yds
4 skeins

Super Fine weight

F 310 (340, 360) yds
3 oz

Sewing machine with
zigzag capability

Tapestry needle

Removable stitch markers

Crochet hook 3.5mm/E-4

3 1¼" buttons

THE WOVEN FABRIC: WARP I, CENTER PANELS

Requirements for 10-dent heddle

Width in heddle	7¼"
Total warp threads	72
Loom waste	24"
Warp length	80"

Warp order

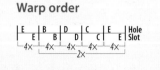

Weft order

Alternate 1 weft pick B with 1 pick F for 24". Weave
4 weft picks each E, C, D, B, E, B, D, and C, then 12
picks E. Place removable stitch marker at each edge.
Alternate 1 weft pick B with 1 pick F for 23½". Weave
8 picks each E, B, D, and C, then 16 picks E.

WEAVING THE FABRIC: WARP I

Warp loom. Wind a shuttle
with each color. Weave,
following the Weft Order for
Warp I. Remove from loom;
zigzag raw edges.

Measurements

	On the loom	Finished fabric

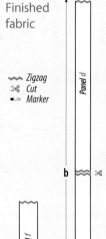
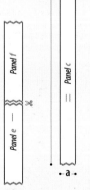

Zigzag
Cut
Marker

Warp I

a	On the loom	6½"
	Finished fabric	6"
b	On the loom	56"
	Off the loom	54"
	Finished fabric	52"

Warp II

a	On the loom	5"
	Finished fabric	4½"
b	On the loom	120"
	Off the loom	114"
	Finished fabric	110"

DESIGN CONCEPT

Working in panels allows for an interplay of warp and weft order. The panels are stitched together on the right side, which creates an additional textural detail. Using the materials indicated makes a lovely, lightweight cover-up for summer nights. Make it in a soft, cozy wool for a cold-weather wrap.

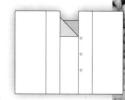

THE WOVEN FABRIC: WARP II, INNER PANELS

Requirements for 10-dent heddle

Width in heddle	5½"
Total warp threads	54
Loom waste	24"
Warp length	144"

Weft order

Alternate 1 weft pick A with 1 pick F.

Warp order

A E A D A D A B A D A C A D A	A E A	Hole
A E A D A B A D A C A D	A E A A	Slot

2x

If Direct Warping this striped warp, carry color A across; cut others between stripes (page 6).

WEAVING THE FABRIC: WARP II

Warp loom. Wind a shuttle with A and another with F. Following the Weft Order for Warp II, weave until piece measures at least 120". Remove from loom; zigzag raw edges.

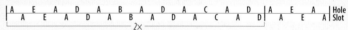

BERROCO Fuji in color

A 9203 Sandy

BERROCO Captiva in colors

B 5547 Fig   **C** 5542 Antique Copper

D 5540 Mascarpone   **E** 5534 Notte

SILK CITY FIBERS Bambu 7 in color

F 360 Onyx

THE WOVEN FABRIC: WARP III, SIDE PANELS

Requirements for 10-dent heddle

	S	M	L
Width in heddle	13¾"	16¼"	18½"
Total warp threads	138	162	186
FOR ALL SIZES			
Loom waste	24"		
Warp length	144"		

Warp order

```
E D A D A D E B A B A B E C A C A C E   E D A D A D E B A B A B E   Hole
  E D A D A D E B A B A B E C A C A C E   E D A D A D E B A B A B E   Slot
                    5 (6,7)×
```

If Direct Warping, carry colors A and E; cut others.

Weft order

[Alternate 1 weft pick A with 1 pick F for 18". Weave (8 picks each E, B, D, and C) 6 times, 8 E. Alternate 1 pick A with 1 pick F for 18"] twice.

Warp III		S	M	L
a	On the loom	11¾"	14¼"	16½"
	Finished fabric	10¼"	12¾"	15"
	ALL SIZES			
b	On the loom	120"		
	Off the loom	114"		
	Finished fabric	110"		

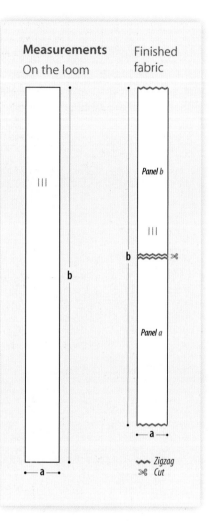

Measurements
On the loom — Finished fabric

III

Panel b

III

b

Panel a

a — a

~~ Zigzag
✄ Cut

WEAVING THE FABRIC: WARP III

Warp loom. Wind a shuttle for each color. Weave, following the Weft Order for Warp III. Remove from loom; zigzag raw edges.

FINISHING THE FABRIC: WARPS I, II, AND III

Hand wash all pieces in lukewarm water with a little agitation. Use spin cycle or wrap in a towel to remove excess water. Place in dryer on low heat until almost dry. Hang until completely dry. Zigzag and cut as shown: Warp I at markers, Warps II and III at centers.

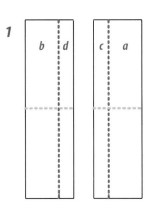

1

b | d   c | a

PUTTING IT ALL TOGETHER

Fold ¾" at neck edge of Panel *e* (4-weft horizontal stripes) to WS, turn under edge, then hem (page 15). Repeat for Panel *f* (8-row weft stripes) EXCEPT fold to RS.

With WS together, tapestry needle, F, and working between the first and second warp threads, sew using Back Stitch (page 15) on RS as follows:

1 Sew Panel *a* to Panel *c* and Panel *b* to Panel *d*. Fold pieces in half lengthwise to locate shoulders.

2 Place Panel *e* 2¼" below shoulder line and sew to Panels *c* and *d*.

3 Place Panel *f* 2¼" below shoulder line and sew to Panel *d*.

Try on and shorten to desired length, allowing 1" for hem. Fold front and back bottom edges to WS, turn under edges, then hem.

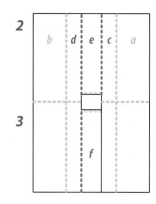

2

3

b d e c a

- - - *Seam*
······ *Single crochet*
ᗧᗧᗧ *Hem on WS*
  ○ *Button*

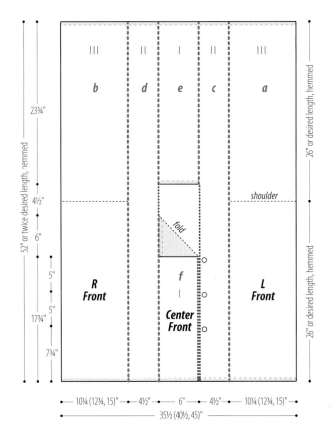

FINISHING THE RUANA

With RS facing, crochet hook, and E, work 2 rows of single crochet (page 10) along edge of Panel *c* from back neck to front hem. Work 2 rows of single crochet along neck edge of Panel *d*.

LAPEL Fold corner of Panel *f* to RS as shown and stitch to edge of Panel *d*, aligning checks with vertical stripes.

BUTTONS AND BUTTONHOLES Lay out fronts, matching hems and aligning edges of Panels *f* and *c*. Mark button and buttonhole placement, placing first at corner of lapel fold and 2 others approximately 5" apart. With RS facing, work 1 row of single crochet along edge of Panel *f* from hem to lapel, turn. **[Chain 10, skip 3 single crochets, single crochet into next single crochet, work to next marker]** twice, chain 10, skip 3 single crochets, single crochet into next single crochet, single crochet to end. Cut yarn and fasten off. Sew buttons 2" from front edge.

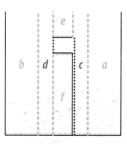

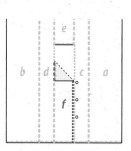

Liquid gold

THE WOVEN FABRIC

Requirements for **12-** OR **12.5-dent heddle**
Width in heddle   16¾"/16"
Total warp threads   202
Loom waste   24"
Warp length   112"

Warp order

Weft order
Alternate 1 weft pick F with 1 pick G.

WEAVING THE FABRIC
Warp loom. Weave enough heading in waste yarn so you will have at least 8" of fringe. Wind a shuttle with E and another with F. Following the Weft Order, weave until piece measures at least 88". Leaving 8" for fringe, remove from loom — untie knots from front apron; do not cut. Remove waste yarn and twist fringe (page 9) for 5", then tie an overhand knot to secure twist; do not trim fringe.

FINISHING THE FABRIC
Hand wash and lay flat to dry.

PUTTING IT ALL TOGETHER
PIECE 1 Measure 46" from one fringed end of fabric. Mark, zigzag, and cut as shown.

PIECE 2 Do this calculation:
46" (length of Piece 1) – **14**/13½" (width of Piece 2) = **32**/32½" (length of Piece 2). Measure **32**/32½" from other fringed end of fabric. Mark, zigzag, and cut.

Fold 1" to WS at raw edge of Pieces 1 and 2, turn under edge, then hem (page 15).

Pin hemmed edge of Piece 2 to RS edge of Piece 1 as shown. With tapestry needle and G, sew together using Blind Stitch and Baseball Stitch (page 15). Trim fringe to desired length.

Measurements

On the loom   Finished fabric

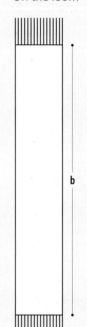 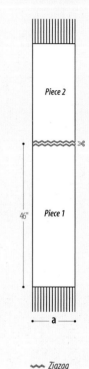

Piece 2

b

46"   Piece 1

a

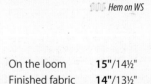

~~~~ Zigzag
✀ Cut
--- Seam
Hem on WS

		On the loom	15"/14½"
a	On the loom		15"/14½"
	Finished fabric		**14"/13½"**
b	On the loom		88"
	Off the loom		83"
	Finished fabric		79"

DESIGN CONCEPT

Two pieces are sewn together to form a point at the back. The construction provides some interesting design possibilities. I like the way the warp stripes meet when the pieces are sewn together. The rayon tape, along with silk, bamboo, and merino yarns, yields a fabric with nice warmth and incredible drape.

Piece 2

Piece 1

31" hemmed

45" hemmed

14"/13½"

A PRISM YARNS Bon Bon in color 307 Gold

MANOS DEL URUGUAY Silk Blend in colors

B 3008 Black   **C** 3043 Juniper

D BERROCO Captiva in color 5534 Notte

E HABU TEXTILES Wrapped Merino in color 6 Teal

F HABU TEXTILES Lace Bamboo in color 7 Teal

G SILK CITY FIBERS Bambu 7 in color 360 Onyx

Shawl-collared ruana

One size

37" wide × 29½" long

12- OR 12.5-dent heddle
20" minimum width

2 shuttles

1"

12

12 OR 12.5

12 OR 12.5 warp threads
and 12 weft threads in plain
weave, on the loom

Light weight

A 750 yds
5 skeins

B 70 yds
1 skein

C 130 yds
1 skein

D 45 yds
1 skein

E 145 yds
1 skein

Medium weight

F 230 yds
3 skeins

Super Fine weight

G 1350 yds
10.2 oz

&

Sewing machine with
zigzag capability

Sewing needle
and thread

Tapestry needle

THE WOVEN FABRIC: WARPS I AND II, BODY

Requirements for **12-** OR 12.5-dent heddle

Width in heddle	**19¾"**/20"
Total warp threads	**238**/250
Loom waste	24"
Warp length	94"

Weft order

Alternate 1 weft pick A with
1 pick G.

Warp order

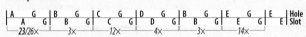

WEAVING THE FABRIC: WARPS I AND II

Warp loom. Wind a shuttle with A and another with G. Following the Weft Order for Warps I and II, weave until piece measures at least 70". Remove from loom; zigzag raw edges. Re-warp loom and weave Warp II to match.

Measurements

On the loom   Finished fabric

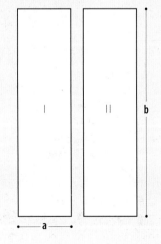

〰 *Zigzag*

Warps I and II

a   On the loom   18"
       Finished fabric   16½"

b   On the loom   70"
       Off the loom   62"
       Finished fabric   61"

DESIGN CONCEPT

A ruana is typically made of 2 rectangles sewn together in the back. That's it. I added a center back panel and a shawl collar. The center panel provides room for the neck, and the shawl collar is a nice design element that, if woven or possibly knit in a soft, comfy yarn, provides warmth and comfort around the neck.

The color-and-weave pattern makes the plain weave look very complicated. Introducing a space-dyed color in the warp makes for an even more complex look. There is nothing plain about this plain weave!

THE WOVEN FABRIC: WARP III, CENTER PANEL/COLLAR

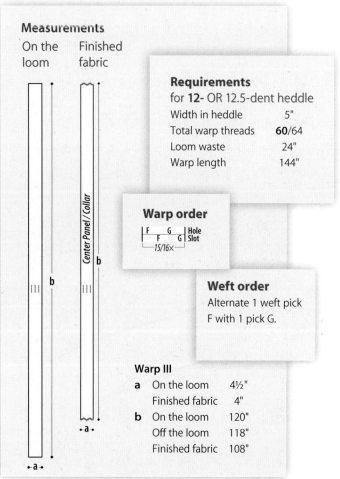

Measurements

On the loom

Finished fabric

Center Panel / Collar

Requirements

for **12-** OR 12.5-dent heddle

Width in heddle	5"
Total warp threads	**60/64**
Loom waste	24"
Warp length	144"

Warp order

	F		G	Hole
	F	G		Slot

15/16×

Weft order

Alternate 1 weft pick F with 1 pick G.

Warp III

a	On the loom	4½"
	Finished fabric	4"
b	On the loom	120"
	Off the loom	118"
	Finished fabric	108"

WEAVING THE FABRIC: WARP III

Warp loom. Wind a shuttle with F and another with G. Following the Weft Order for Warp III, weave until piece measures at least 120". Remove from loom; zigzag raw edges.

FINISHING THE FABRIC

Hand wash all pieces in lukewarm water. Use spin cycle or wrap in a towel to remove excess water. Drape over bar to dry.

MANOS DEL URUGUAY Silk Blend in colors

A 3043 Juniper   **B** 3008 Black

C 300U Rust   **D** 3068 Citric   **E** 3110 Stellar

F BERROCO Captiva in color 5534 Notte

G SILK CITY FIBERS Bambu 7 in color 360 Onyx

PUTTING IT ALL TOGETHER

Fold Panels 1 and 2 in half lengthwise. Measure length from fold (shoulder) to raw edge. Mark off a length of center panel to this measurement. Zigzag and cut as shown. Set aside the remaining piece for the collar.

Fold 1" along one raw edge to WS, turn under edge, then hem (page 15). With hemmed edge at neck, pin piece between Panels 1 and 2, ending 1" down from shoulder. With tapestry needle and G, sew to edges of Panels 1 and 2 using Baseball Stitch (page 15).

SHAWL COLLAR AND HEM Pin collar to Panels 1 and 2 along one center front edge, across back neck, and along other center front edge. Follow Steps 1–3 to attach collar and hem garment.

ARMHOLES Measure 9" from shoulder seams and mark side edges for armholes. At markers, join fronts to back with a few Overhand stitches (page 15). Fasten well OR continue sewing sides closed using Baseball Stitch.

Shawl collar and hem

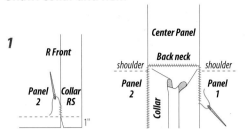

1

Starting and ending 1" from bottom edge, sew collar in place using Baseball Stitch.

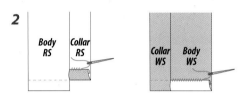

2

At ends of collar, fold 1" to RS, turn under edge, then hem.

Flip garment over and fold 1" body hem to WS, turn under edge, then hem.

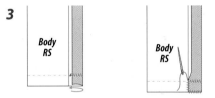

3

Fold collar to RS so the outer edge meets the body/collar seam.

Stitch along bottom and side edges of folded hem.

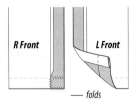

— *folds*

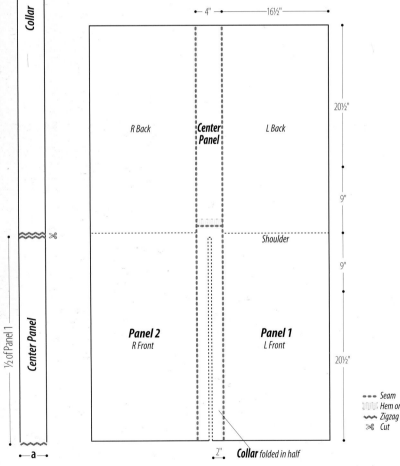

Legend:
- --- *Seam*
- ⊓⊓⊓ *Hem on WS*
- ∿∿ *Zigzag*
- ✂ *Cut*

Collar *folded in half*

PULLOVERS

Olive garden tunic

S (M, L, 1X)

Shown in SMALL, page 47

A 41 (44, 48, 51)"
B 27" maximum length;
shorten as desired.
C 18½ (19, 20, 21)"

10-dent heddle
10" minimum width

3 shuttles

10 warp threads and
10 weft threads in plain
weave, on the loom

Light weight

A 550 (580, 610, 640) yds
5 skeins

B 340 (360, 370, 380) yds
3 skeins

C 220 (220, 230, 230) yds
2 skeins

D 50 (50, 50, 70) yds
1 skein

Weaving yarn

E 130 (140, 150, 160) yds
1 cone

Sewing machine with
zigzag capability

THE WOVEN FABRIC: WARP I, CENTER PANELS

Requirements for 10-dent heddle

Width in heddle	10"
Total warp threads	100
Loom waste	24"
Warp length	84"

Warp order

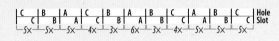

Weft order

[8 weft picks A, (1 pick C, 1 pick A) 6 times, 8 picks C, (1 pick B, 1 pick C) 6 times, 8 picks B, (1 pick A, 1 pick B) 6 times].

WEAVING THE FABRIC: WARP I

Warp loom. Wind a shuttle each with A, B, and C. Following the Weft Order, weave until piece measures at least 60". Remove from loom; zigzag raw edges.

WEAVING THE FABRIC: WARP II

Warp loom. Wind a shuttle with A and weave until piece measures at least 120". Remove from loom; zigzag raw edges.

FINISHING THE FABRIC: WARPS I AND II

Hand wash, roll in towel to remove excess water, and place in dryer on low heat until almost dry. Hang or lay flat until completely dry. Zigzag and cut each piece into 2 equal lengths as shown: 2 center panels and 2 side panels.

Measurements

On the loom	Finished fabric

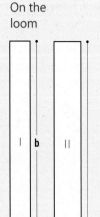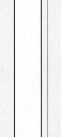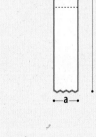

〰 *Zigzag*
✄ *Cut*

Warp I	ALL SIZES
a On the loom	9½"
Finished fabric	9"
b On the loom	60"
Off the loom	57"
Finished fabric	54"

Warp II	S	M	L	1X
a On the loom	8"	8½"	9"	9½"
Finished fabric	7½"	8"	8½"	9"

	ALL SIZES
b On the loom	120"
Off the loom	114"
Finished fabric	108"

DESIGN CONCEPT

Designing with panels allows for combining different warp and weft patterns. For this design, it also provided the ability to shape the neck without having to do any cutting. Sleeves are knit using a slip-stitch pattern that mimics the look of the weaving. Side slits make a long tunic easier to pull on and add to the comfort factor.

TWISTED SISTERS Essential in colors

A Brazzle

B Willow

C Lemongrass

D Alba

E BORGS Cottolin 22/2 in Black

THE WOVEN FABRIC: WARP II, SIDE PANELS

Requirements for 10-dent heddle

	S	M	L	1X
Width in heddle	8½"	9"	9½"	10"
Total warp threads	84	90	96	102

FOR ALL SIZES
Loom waste	24"
Warp length	144"

Warp order

Weft order
Weave with A.

PUK

[Pick up and knit a stitch, skip 2 weft threads] to end (page 10). Count stitches and increase or decrease to required number on the next row.

HALF-LINEN STITCH

MULTIPLE OF 2 + 1
SI 1 *Slip 1 purlwise with yarn at RS of work.*
Rows 1 and 3 (WS) Purl.
Row 2 K1, **[sl 1, k1]** to end.
Row 4 K1, **[k1, sl 1]** to last stitch, k1.
Repeat Rows 1–4.

DEC 1

At beginning of RS rows K1, k2tog.
At end of RS rows SSK, k1.

4mm/US6, 60cm (24") long

10cm/4"

36 ⊞ 21

over Half-linen Stitch

Sewing needle and thread

See Knitting Basics on page 10 for unfamiliar techniques.

Side Panel   Side Panel

1"
1"

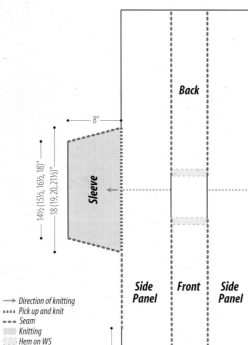

→ Direction of knitting
•••• Pick up and knit
--- Seam
▨ Knitting
▨ Hem on WS

Back

Sleeve   Sleeve

Side Panel   Front   Side Panel

8"

14½ (15½, 16½, 18")
18 (19, 20, 21½)"

8"

7½ (8, 8½, 9)"
5½ (6, 7, 7½)"
20½ (22, 24, 25½)"

PUTTING IT ALL TOGETHER

1 Place side panels side by side so the stripes mirror.
With RS together, fold each panel in half lengthwise to locate shoulders. Baste and sew 1" darts at shoulders.

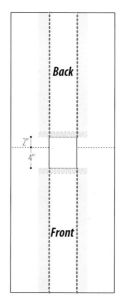

Back

Front

6"

neck width
5½ (6, 7, 7½)"

Back

Front

2"
4"

2 Fold ¾" along one end of one center panel to WS for back neck. Fold 1¾" along one end of the other center panel to WS for front neck. Turn edges under, then hem. Mark center 5½ (6, 7, 7½)" neck width on both panels. Place panels face up with neck edges 6" apart.

3 Pin side panels on top of center panels, aligning side panel edges with neck markers; top of front panel edge should be 4" down from shoulder seam and top of back panel edge should be 2" down from shoulder seam. Join panels by machine or using Back Stitch (page 15) close to the edges of the side panels.

KNITTING THE SLEEVES

Measure 9 (9½, 10, 10¾)" from shoulder seams and mark side edges. With RS facing and B, pick up and knit (PUK) between markers. **Begin Half-linen Stitch: Row 1** Purl, adjusting to 95 (101, 107, 113) stitches. Dec 1 each side every 4 rows 9 times, end with a WS row — 77 (83, 89, 95) stitches. **Next row** (RS) Change to A and continue in pattern until sleeve measures 8" or desired length, end with a WS row. Bind off.

FINISHING THE TUNIC

Sew sleeve seams. With A, sew side seams using Baseball Stitch (page 15), leaving bottom 8" open. Turn edges of side slits to WS, then hem. Try on and mark finished length. Allowing ¾" hem allowance, zigzag and trim excess fabric. Fold to WS, turn under edge, then hem. Turn under side edges of neckline, then hem.

Hand wash piece again. Lay flat to dry. Steam press.

One size

A 31½"/30" across back
B Maximum length 26";
shorten as desired
C 15¾"/15"

12- OR 12.5-dent heddle
15" minimum width

4 shuttles

1"

12
12 OR 12.5

12 OR 12.5 warp threads
and 12 weft threads in plain
weave, on the loom using
A, B, or C; 24 weft threads
using D

Fine weight

A 560 yds
4 skeins

C 465 yds
3 skeins

Super Fine weight

B 490 yds
4 oz

Weaving yarn

D 190 yds
1 skein

&

Waste yarn

Sewing machine with
zigzag capability

Sewing needle and thread

Tapestry needle

Embroidery needle

DMC Cotton Embroidery
Floss: 2 skeins 3731 Dark
Dusty Rose (E1) and 1 skein
each 3740 Dark Antique
Violet (E2), 729 Gold (E3),
3743 Lilac (E4), and 301
Terra Cotta (E5)

Pontunic

THE WOVEN FABRIC: WARP I, SIDE PANELS

Requirements for **12-** OR **12.5-dent heddle**
Width in heddle   **12¼"/11¾"**
Total warp threads   148
Loom waste   24"
Warp length   144"

Warp order

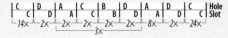

Weft order

Alternate 1 weft pick A with 1 pick B.

WEAVING THE FABRIC: WARP I

Warp loom. Wind a shuttle with A and another with B.
Following the Weft Order for Warp I, weave until piece
measures at least 120". Remove from loom; zigzag and cut
into 2 equal lengths as shown.

FINISHING THE FABRIC: WARPS I AND II

Hand wash with some agitation. Rinse and wrap in towel to
remove excess water. Place in dryer on low heat for about 10
minutes. Lay flat until completely dry. Steam press.

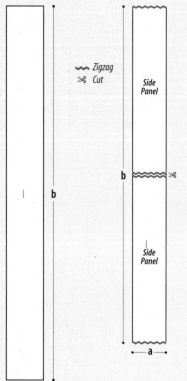

Measurements
On the loom   Finished fabric

Zigzag
Cut

Side Panel

b

Side Panel

a

Warp I
a   On the loom   11¼"/10¾"
      Finished fabric   **11"**/10½"
b   On the loom   120"
      Off the loom   113"
      Finished fabric   108"

DESIGN CONCEPT

It's a poncho…it's a tunic…it's a pontunic! Woven in straight panels that are then stitched together, it is reminiscent of peasant shirts popular in Mexico and South America. I warped the loom twice so I could have a different warp-stripe pattern in the center and side panels. The center panels are decorated with cross stitch, worked while the weaving is under tension on the loom. Follow my charts or work out your own designs on graph paper.

A MANOS DEL URUGUAY Serena in color 9710 Alpine

B SILK CITY FIBERS Bambu 7 in color 285 Mint

C CLASSIC ELITE Firefly in color 7757 Chicory

D REDFISH DYEWORKS 20/2 Silk in color RPbl4b Eggplant

THE WOVEN FABRIC: WARP II, CENTER PANELS

Requirements
for **12-** OR 12.5-dent heddle

Width in heddle	**12¼"**/11¾"
Total warp ends	148
Loom waste	24"
Warp length	80"

Warp order

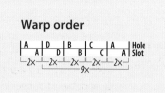

Weft order

Alternate 1 weft pick A with 1 pick B until piece measures 23" for back (21" for front). Weave **[4 picks C, 4 picks B, 8 picks D, 4 picks A]** 3 times for back (4 times for front), end 12 picks C.

Measurements

On the loom   Finished fabric

1"

~~~ Zigzag
✂ Cut
▓ Waste yarn

Front Panel

Back Panel

Warp II

a	On the loom	**11¼"**/10¾"
	Finished fabric	**11"**/10½"
b	On the loom	28"
	Off the loom	27"
	Finished fabric	26"
c	On the loom	25"
	Off the loom	24"
	Finished fabric	23"

Cross stitch

A cross stitch is made in two steps: a diagonal stitch to the right, crossed by a diagonal stitch to the left. Work each cross stitch over 4 warp threads and 4 weft threads of the woven checkerboard pattern.

TO WORK CROSS STITCH ON THE LOOM:
Using all 6 strands of embroidery floss held together, cut a piece 2 yards long. Thread through embroidery needle and, using floss doubled (12 strands), work cross stitch chart over woven checkerboard pattern. Leave long ends hanging in back to weave in and secure after weaving is off the loom.

WEAVING THE FABRIC: WARP II

Warp loom. Wind a shuttle with each color. Following the Weft Order for Warp II, weave back panel. Work Back Cross Stitch chart. Weave 1" waste. Following the Weft Order for Warp II, weave front panel. Work Front Cross Stitch chart. Remove from loom; zigzag and cut pieces apart.

Front cross stitch

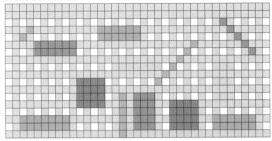

Back cross stitch

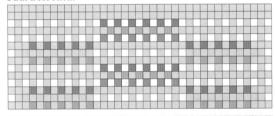

■ E1	☐☐ WOVEN CHECK
■ E2	4 warp threads
	×4 weft threads
☐ E3	in A, B, or C
	OR
■ E4	4 warp threads
■ E5	×8 weft threads in D

Overhand stitch

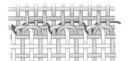

1 Overlap edges.
2 Working from right to left, insert needle through the fabric from back to front, weaving up and over second loop of overlapping pair of loops...
3 ...then under 4 threads of underlying fabric.
4 Repeat.

PUTTING IT ALL TOGETHER

Turn under top edges of center panels, then hem (page 15).

Find center of each side panel and mark shoulders at neck edge. Measure 3" down from marker and pin front panel in place; side panels overlap front panel by 8 warp threads. With RS facing, C, and tapestry needle, sew panels in place using Overhand Stitch (see drawing), leaving the scalloped edge exposed. Repeat for back panel EXCEPT measure 2" down from marker.

Try on and pin hem to desired length. Zigzag; trim away excess fabric if necessary. Turn under edge, then hem. Steam press.

With C and tapestry needle, overlap side edges and sew together, leaving 12" open below shoulder for armholes.

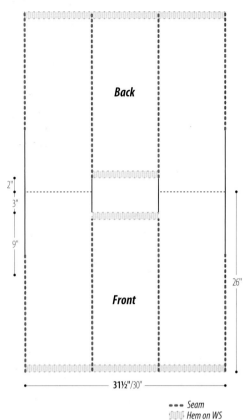

■■■ Seam
〰〰 Hem on WS

If you prefer, chart your own cross stitch.

Your front cross stitch

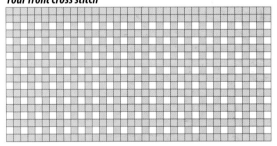

Your back cross stitch

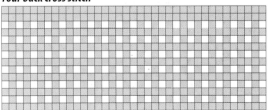

53

Aegean tunic

WEAVING
KNITTING
SEWING

LOOSE FIT

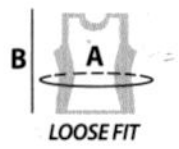

XS (S, M, L, 1X)
Shown in SMALL, page 55
A 40½ (43½, 46½, 50, 53)"
B 24 (25, 26, 27, 28)"

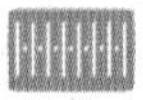

THE WOVEN FABRIC: WARP I, LEFT FRONT AND BACK

Requirements for 10-dent heddle

	XS	S	M	L	1X
Width in heddle	15½"	16½"	17¼"	18	18¾"
Working warp threads	156	164	172	180	188

FOR ALL SIZES	
Loom waste	24"
Warp length	96"

Weft order

Alternate a single strand of A with a single strand of B.

Warp order

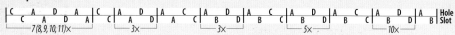

A and B remain doubled in the warp; C and D are treated as usual.

10-dent heddle
20" minimum width

2 shuttles

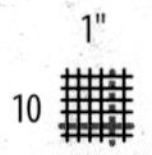

1"
10
10
10 warp threads and
10 weft threads in plain
weave, on the loom

1 4

Super Fine weight
A 470 (500, 530, 550,
580) yds
1 skein

B 570 (610, 640, 670,
710) yds
1 (1, 2, 2, 2) skeins

Medium weight
C 160 (180, 200, 220,
245) yds
1 skein

D 170 (180, 180, 190,
190) yds
1 skein

Sewing machine with
zigzag capability

Example: When threading the first 2 sections of the Warp Order (reading from right to left), work as follows: loop B through first slot, loop A through hole, **[loop D through slot, skip a hole, loop B through slot, loop A through hole]** 10 times. After winding onto the back beam and cutting the loops, the doubled threads of A and B remain in the slot or hole; remove 1 D thread from slot and pull through hole next to it.

WEAVING THE FABRIC: WARP I

Warp loom. After weaving heading, make a butterfly (page 26) with a single strand of B and work 1 row of Hemstitch (page 9). Using single strands of yarn, wind a shuttle with A and another with B. Alternating A and B, weave until piece measures at least 72"; end with 1 row of Hemstitch. Remove from loom, leaving a few inches of fringe at top and bottom edges.

WEAVING THE FABRIC: WARP II

Warp loom. Wind a shuttle with B. Using B only, hemstitch and weave as for Warp I.

FINISHING THE FABRIC: WARPS I AND II

Hand wash both pieces and hang to dry.

Zigzag and cut each piece into 2 equal lengths as shown. Trim fringe at hemstitched edge to ½".

Measurements

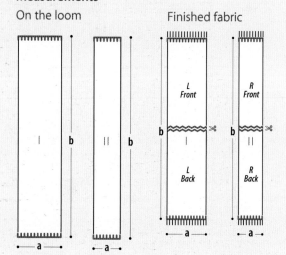

On the loom   Finished fabric

L Front   R Front
L Back   R Back

〰 *Zigzag*
✂ *Cut*
⊔⊔⊔ *Hemstitch on loom*

Warp I

	XS	S	M	L	1X
a On the loom	14¼"	15¼"	16"	16¾"	17½"
Finished fabric	13"	14"	14¾"	15½"	16¼"

ALL SIZES	
b On the loom	72"
Off the loom	66"
Finished fabric	58"

Warp II

	XS	S	M	L	1X
a On the loom	7½"	8¼"	9"	9¾"	10½"
Finished fabric	7¼"	8"	8¾"	9½"	10¼"

ALL SIZES	
b On the loom	72"
Off the loom	66"
Finished fabric	58"

DESIGN CONCEPT

Weaving two panels, one wider than the other, creates an asymmetrical look. Folded corners shape the neckline and armhole — no cutting is required. If desired, button tabs cinch in the waist.

I designed the stripes so the colors would blend together like the sea, using a knitting design program to help me visualize the results. Of course it's not a perfect vision, as the yarns I used were hand-dyed and shaded and created their own pattern.

Sometimes you just have to have fringe! The bottom edges are hemstitched on the loom to secure the edge from unraveling.

THE WOVEN FABRIC:
WARP II, RIGHT FRONT AND BACK

Requirements for 10-dent heddle

	XS	S	M	L	1X
Width in heddle	8"	8¾"	9½"	10¼"	11"
Working warp threads	80	88	96	104	112
FOR ALL SIZES					
Loom waste	24"				
Warp length	96"				

Warp order

B	C		B	C	C		B	C	C	C	C		B	**Hole**
	B		C	B	C	C	C	B	C	C	C	C	C	B	**Slot**

3×   3×   6 (7, 8, 9, 10)×

See note for Warp I; B remains doubled.

Weft order
Weave a single strand of B.

MOUNTAIN COLORS HALF CREPE IN COLORS

A HARMONY SWEETGRASS

B BIG SKY

C MOUNTAIN COLORS MERINO RIBBON IN COLOR HARMONY ASPEN

D LANG YARNS SOL DÉGRADÉ IN COLOR 783.0044 GREENS

weave • knit • wear

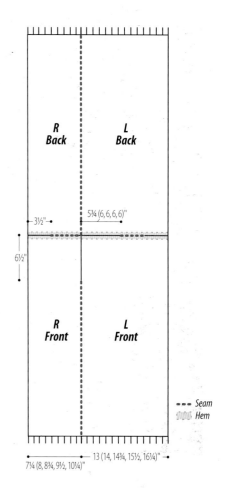

PUTTING IT ALL TOGETHER

Back

With RS together and using Back Stitch (page 15), sew back piece of Warp I to back piece of Warp II, matching fringed edges and checking that stripes follow the Stripe Plan.

HEM Try on and mark finished length. To maintain fringe at bottom edge, make length adjustments at top edge. Allowing ¾" for hem, zigzag, trim away excess fabric, and fold hem to WS. Turn under edge, then hem. Mark center of hemmed edge for center back neck.

Front

Shorten front panels to same length as back. Sew front panels together from fringe to 6½" below top edge using Baseball Stitch (page 15). With RS together, sew right shoulder seam with Blind Stitch (page 15), beginning 3½" from armhole edge and sewing to end of right front. Measure seam and duplicate at left shoulder, beginning 3½" from armhole edge.

ARMHOLES Mark 9 (10, 11, 12, 12)" down from each shoulder seam on front and back. With WS together and using Back Stitch, sew side seams from markers to bottom edge. Fold corners of shoulders to inside and sew in place.

Sew buttons at waist as shown on schematic. Sew 6 buttons along front seam, with 1 at neck opening, 1 at bottom, and the rest spaced evenly between. Allow front neck corner to fold down.

4mm/US6

Sewing needle and thread

Tapestry needle

10 19mm (¾") buttons

See Knitting Basics on page 10 for unfamiliar techniques.

KNITTING THE BUTTONBAND

With D, cast on 94 (100, 106, 112, 118).

Row 1 (RS) K1, **[k2, pass second stitch over first, k1, pass second stitch over first]** to end.

Row 2 K1, **[cast on 2, k1]** to end. Bind off. Button onto front-seam buttons.

KNITTING THE BUTTON TABS

MAKE 2

With D, cast on 16. Work Rows 1–2 of buttonband. Bind off. Button onto waist buttons.

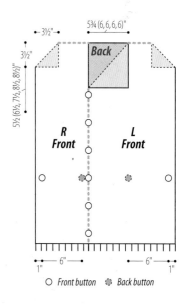

○ *Front button*   ❀ *Back button*

Cleo's cover

LOOSE FIT

S–M (L, 1X)
Shown in SMALL–MEDIUM,
page 59

A 42 (46, 48)"/
40½ (44, 46)"
B 21 (22, 23)"

12- OR 12.5-dent heddle
20" minimum width

* Width measurements are
given for 12-dent heddle
and will be approximately
¾" less for 12.5-dent heddle

2 shuttles

1"

12
12 OR 12.5

12 OR 12.5 warp threads
and 12 weft threads in plain
weave, on the loom

Fine weight
A 50 (60, 60) yds
1 skein

B 60 (60, 70) yds
1 skein

C 210 (230, 240) yds
2 skeins

D 330 (340, 370) yds
3 skeins

E 80 (90, 90) yds
1 skein

Super Fine weight
F 430 (480, 500) yds
4 oz

&

Sewing machine with
zigzag capability
Removable stitch markers

THE WOVEN FABRIC

Requirements for 12- OR 12.5-dent heddle

	S–M	L	1X
* Width in heddle	17"	19"	20"
Total warp threads	204	228	240
FOR ALL SIZES			
Loom waste	24"		
Warp length	84"		

Warp order

Weft order
Alternate 1 weft pick C with 1 pick F.

WEAVING THE FABRIC
Warp loom. Wind a shuttle with C and another with F. Following the
Weft Order, weave until piece measures at least 60". Remove from
loom; zigzag raw edges. Place removable stitch marker at each end.

FINISHING THE FABRIC
Hand wash. Zigzag and cut into 2 equal lengths as shown.

Measurements
On the loom   Finished fabric

Back

b

Front   27"

a

〜〜 Zigzag
✄ Cut
🡆 Removable marker

	S–M	L	1X
* **a** On the loom	15½"	17½"	18½"
Finished fabric	14"	16"	17"
	ALL SIZES		
b On the loom	60"		
Off the loom	57"		
Finished fabric	54"		

DESIGN CONCEPT

Two straight panels are woven; knit gussets are added for shoulder shaping. Lacy side panels make for a delicate, dressy little blouse. Alternating a thin bamboo yarn with a linen blend in the warp and the weft creates a fabric with lovely drape. Wear it loose or cinched with a belt.

CLASSIC ELITE YARNS FIREFLY IN COLORS

A 7781 SOUR APPLE

B 7735 CAPRI

C 7794 PISTACHIO

D 7766 SICILY

E 7746 MERMAID

F SILK CITY FIBERS BAMBU 7 IN COLOR 300 WILLOW

PUK
[Pick up and knit a stitch, skip 2 weft threads] to end (page 10).

PUTTING IT ALL TOGETHER
A marker indicates bottom edge of each piece. Fold ¾" at other end of each piece to WS, turn under edge, then hem.

KNITTING THE SHOULDERS
Mark front and back top edges 2½ (3½, 4)" in from side edges.

FRONT LEFT SHOULDER With double-pointed needles (dpns), RS facing, and C, PUK 18 (21, 24) from side edge to marker. Knit 2 rows. **Begin short rows: Next 2 rows** (WS) Knit to last 2 (3, 4), W&T; knit to end. **[Knit to 2 (3, 4) before last wrap, W&T; knit to end]** 3 times. **Next row** Knit all stitches, hiding wraps; leave stitches on needle.

BACK LEFT SHOULDER PUK 18 (21, 24) from marker to side edge and work short rows as for front left shoulder EXCEPT on RS rows. Knit 1 row. Join left shoulder using 3-Needle Bind-Off (page 11). Work front right shoulder as for back left shoulder and back right shoulder as for front left shoulder. Join right shoulder.
Try on and mark finished length. Allowing 1" for hem allowance, zigzag; trim away excess fabric if necessary. Fold to WS, turn under edge, then hem (page 15).

KNITTING THE SIDE PANELS *MAKE 4*
With D, cast on 18. Work Rows 1–10 of Panel Lace 17 (18, 19) times, or until piece, slightly stretched, measures length from hemmed bottom edge to shoulder seam, end having worked Row 9. Bind off.

FINISHING THE TOP
Pin side panels to side edges of front and back, overlapping 2 warp threads of weaving. With D and tapestry needle, sew together using Overcast Stitch (page 15). Sew top edges of knit panels together for 1", leaving slanted edges open.

Steam woven panels but not knit panels. Place damp towel on knit panels and allow to dry.

ARMHOLE Tack edges of knit panels together 11" down from seam at shoulders.

10cm/4"

40

24
over garter stitch

3.75mm/US5

3.75mm/US5

Sewing needle
and thread

Tapestry needle

See Knitting Basics on
page 10 for unfamiliar
techniques.

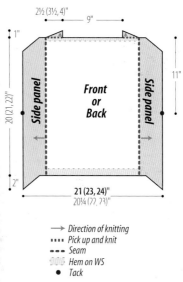

2½ (3½, 4)"
9"
1"
11"
20 (21, 22)"
2"

Side panel

Front
or
Back

Side panel

21 (23, 24)"
20¼ (22, 23)"

→ Direction of knitting
···· Pick up and knit
--- Seam
Hem on WS
● Tack

Panel lace

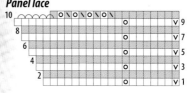

☐ Knit on RS
▦ Knit on WS
⊡ Yarn over (yo)
◩ K2tog on WS
▾ Sl 1 knitwise with
   yarn at WS of work
↷ Bind off

PANEL LACE

SL 1 Slip 1 knitwise with yarn at WS of work.

Row 1 Sl 1, k6, yo, k11. *Row 2* K19.

Row 3 Sl 1, k6, yo, k12. *Row 4* K20.

Row 5 Sl 1, k6, yo, k13. *Row 6* K21.

Row 7 Sl 1, k6, yo, k14. *Row 8* K22.

Row 9 Sl 1, k6, yo, k15.

Row 10 Bind off 5, **[yo, k2tog]** 4 times, k9.

Tweedy shirt

WEAVING

SEWING

B | A
LOOSE FIT

XS (S, M, L, 1X)
Shown in SMALL, page 63

A 44 (46, 49, 52, 54)"
42 (44, 47, 50, 52)"
B Maximum length 24";
shorten as desired

12- OR 12.5-dent heddle
15 (15, 15, 15, 20)"
minimum width
* Width measurements are
given for 12-dent heddle
and will be ½" less for
12.5-dent heddle.

2 shuttles

1"

12 <grid>

12 OR 12.5

12 OR 12.5 warp threads
and 12 weft threads in plain
weave, on the loom

Medium weight
A 200 (200, 210, 220,
230) yds
2 (2, 3, 3, 3) balls
Weaving yarn
B 420 (440, 450, 470,
490) yds
1 (1, 1, 2, 2) cones
C 130 yds 1 skein
Fine weight
D 360 (370, 380, 390,
400) yds
3 balls
E 72 yds 1 ball

Sewing machine with
zigzag capability
Sewing needle and thread
Tapestry needle
1 32mm (1¼") button

THE WOVEN FABRIC

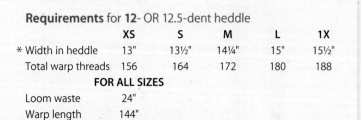

Requirements for **12**- OR 12.5-dent heddle

	XS	S	M	L	1X
* Width in heddle	13"	13½"	14¼"	15"	15½"
Total warp threads	156	164	172	180	188
FOR ALL SIZES					
Loom waste	24"				
Warp length	144"				

Warp order

A C E A B E C A B D E D C D C A B A | Hole
A C E A B E C A B D E D C D C A B A | Slot
4× — 3× — 4× — 3× — 4× — 8× — 3× — — 3× — 5× — 6 (8, 10, 12, 14)×
└ neck edge

Weft order
Alternate 1 weft pick B with 1 pick D.

WEAVING THE FABRIC

Warp loom. Wind a shuttle with B and another with D. Following the
Weft Order, weave until piece measures at least 120". Remove from loom;
zigzag raw edges.

FINISHING THE FABRIC

Hand wash and hang to dry. Steam press.
Zigzag and cut into 4 equal lengths as shown.

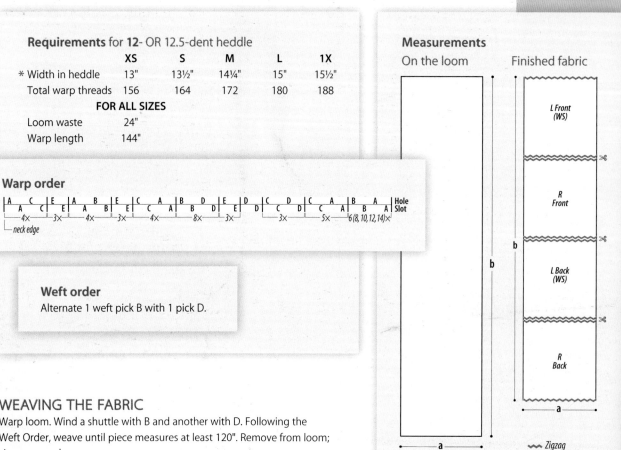

Measurements
On the loom   Finished fabric

L Front
(WS)

R
Front

b

L Back
(WS)

R
Back

b

a

a

〰〰 Zigzag
✂ Cut

		XS	S	M	L	1X
*a	On the loom	12½"	13"	13¾"	14½"	15"
	Finished fabric	11½"	12"	12¾"	13½"	14"
	ALL SIZES					
b	On the loom	120"				
	Off the loom	110"				
	Finished fabric	105"				

DESIGN CONCEPT

The construction is simple: 4 straight panels, hemmed at both top and bottom edges. The pieces overlap in the front and back, and the shoulder seams are left open for a flattering drape. The fronts are partially sewn closed. Add a decorative button or pin.

I obsessed over the stripe design and finally decided to just start warping. I kept most of the interest in the section from the center neck to the shoulder. Yarn A is an ombre yarn that changes in color as well as texture, which provides a more complicated look to the fabric. This top is soft, airy, and silky — perfect for summer!

A TRENDSETTER YARNS Phoenix in color 331 Key Lime

B HABU TEXTILES Tweedy Silk in color 6 Gray Taupe

C REDFISH DYEWORKS 20/2 Silk in color Rbl4b Garnet

D CLASSIC ELITE YARNS Firefly in color 7706 Linum

E HABU TEXTILES Root Sizing Silk Gima in color 8 Grass Yellow

PUTTING IT ALL TOGETHER

Back

Flip one piece over so the neck edge stripes (see Warp Order) meet at the middle; overlap right back over left back for 1". With C, sew pieces together using Back Stitch (page 15) on RS, sewing along a warp thread of the same color and leaving bottom 7" unsewn.

Fold ¾" at top edge to WS, turn under edge, then hem (page 15). Mark center of hemmed edge for center back neck. Mark 4½ (4½, 4¾, 5, 5)" in each direction from center back neck for start of shoulder seam.

Fronts

Flip one piece as for back; fold and hem top edges. Matching stripes at shoulders and beginning at markers, sew shoulder seams using Blind Stitch (page 15) for 2 (2, 2½, 3, 3½)".

Try on and mark finished length. Allowing 1" for hem, zigzag and trim away excess fabric. Fold hem allowance to WS, turn under edge, then hem.

Overlap left front over right front for 1". Beginning 7" down from top, sew as for back, leaving 8" open at the bottom. Sew button through both layers at bottom of neck opening.

With WS together and B, sew side seams on RS between first and second warp threads, using Back Stitch and leaving 8½ (9, 9½, 10, 10½)" open at armholes and 6" open at bottom.

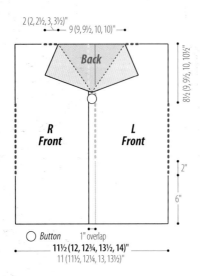

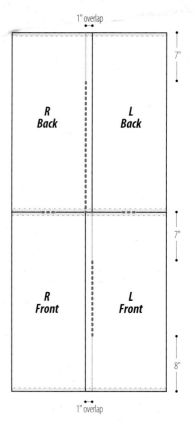

- - - *Seam*

Hem on WS

JACKETS

Mad plaid jacket

WEAVING
KNITTING
SEWING

OVERSIZED FIT

One size
A 56"
B Maximum length of
back from shoulder 24";
shorten as desired.
(Front is shown 2" shorter
than back.)
C 21½"

10-dent heddle
20" minimum width

3 shuttles

10 warp threads and
8 weft threads in plain
weave, on the loom

Medium weight
A 510 yds
4 balls
B 310 yds
4 balls
C 610 yds
8 skeins

Waste yarn

Sewing machine with
zigzag capability

THE WOVEN FABRIC

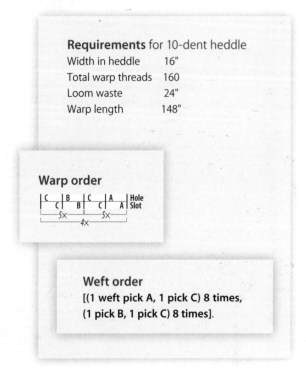

Requirements for 10-dent heddle
Width in heddle   16"
Total warp threads   160
Loom waste   24"
Warp length   148"

Warp order

C	B	C	A	Hole
C	B	C	A	Slot

5x   4x   5x

Weft order
[(1 weft pick A, 1 pick C) 8 times,
(1 pick B, 1 pick C) 8 times].

WEAVING THE FABRIC

Warp loom. Wind a shuttle each with A, B, and C.
∗ Following the Weft Order, weave until piece measures 28", end with
shuttle at right edge.

SHAPE NECK Weave first 40 warp threads for collar (**c**); wind a butterfly
(page 26) with waste yarn and weave remaining 120 threads. Work both
sections for 2", then weave with waste yarn across all warp threads for 1".
Repeat from ∗ 3 more times.

Remove from loom; zigzag and cut as shown.

FINISHING THE FABRIC

Hand wash and lay flat to dry.

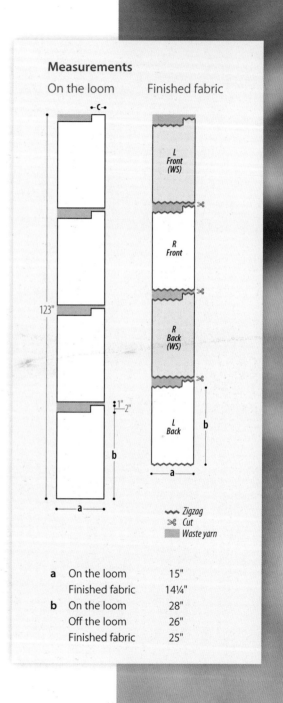

Measurements

On the loom   Finished fabric

123"

| | L Front (WS) |
| R Front |
| R Back (WS) |
| L Back |

~~~ Zigzag
✂ Cut
▨ Waste yarn

a	On the loom	15"
	Finished fabric	14¼"
b	On the loom	28"
	Off the loom	26"
	Finished fabric	25"

DESIGN CONCEPT

*A very evenly woven plaid goes m-a-a-a-d thanks to
3 space-dyed yarns with varied textures. The shape is
a wide rectangle achieved by weaving 2 pieces for the
front and 2 for the back, each with a tab for the collar;
the sleeves are knit. The sample shows the back dipping
2" longer than the front for a swingy jacket. The front and the back could
be the same length, however, and all could be made longer than shown.
If you're not sure what would look best, weave the pieces to the maximum
length indicated, then shorten once you have tried it on.*

A CRYSTAL PALACE YARNS Aria in color 101 Tosca

B TRENDSETTER YARNS Orchidea in color 610 Blueberry Hill

C TRENDSETTER YARNS Twiggy in color 98 Burnt Embers

PUTTING IT ALL TOGETHER

L Back RS

R Back WS

1 Flip right back and place on left back with RS together. Pin, baste, and sew center back seam between third and fourth warp threads (¼" seam allowance). Press seam open, using steam.

2a Lay back down with RS facing up.

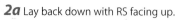

a

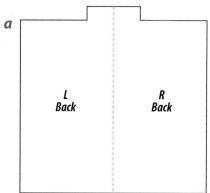

L Back

R Back

3 Turn RS out. With tapestry needle and C, sew side edges of collar together using Baseball Stitch (page 15), leaving 1" at top of collar unsewn.

4 Fold top 1" of back collar to WS, turn under edge, then hem (page 15).

a

5a Fold top 1" of front collar to RS, turn under edges, then hem.

b Neaten and sew top edge of collar seams.

b

3.75mm/US5

10cm/4"

33 18

over stockinette stitch, using A

&

Tapestry needle

Sewing needle and thread

1 1½"–2" button

See Knitting Basics on page 10 for unfamiliar techniques.

b Place left front on left back and right front on right back with RS together. Aligning vertical stripes, pin, baste, and sew shoulder seams on diagonal as shown. Turn under raw edges at shoulder, then hem.

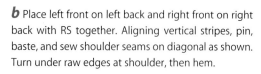

2"

b

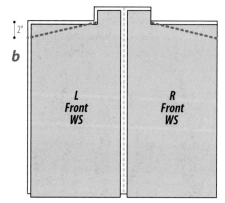

L Front WS

R Front WS

KNITTING THE SLEEVES

Measure 8 (8½, 9)" from shoulder seams and mark side edges. With RS facing and A, pick up and knit (PUK) 72 (77, 81) between markers (page 10). Starting with a knit row (WS) and working in Reverse Stockinette, **[work 3 rows even, Dec 1 each side of next row]** 7 times, then Dec 1 each side of every WS row 9 times — 40 (45, 49) stitches. Work in garter stitch (knit all rows) for 2" or to desired length. Bind off loosely.

FINISHING THE JACKET

Sew side and sleeve seams using Baseball Stitch.

BACK HEM Try on and mark finished length. To shape curve, place pins to mark fold line, then baste along this line and remove pins. Baste another line ¾" below fold line to indicate cutting line. Zigzag a row of stitches along this line and trim away excess fabric. To reduce bulk, trim off bottom corners at seam allowance. Fold to WS along fold line, turn under edge, then hem. Optional: Shorten to an even length around, allowing ¾" for hem.

FRONT EDGES With RS facing and A, PUK along left front edge; count stitches. Knit 2 rows. Bind off. Mark right front edge 7" down from top of collar for buttonhole. PUK same number of stitches along right front edge. Knit to marker, bind off 4, knit to end. **Next row** Knit across, casting on 4 over bound-off stitches. Bind off.

Sew button to left front, opposite buttonhole.

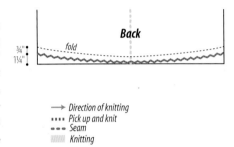

¾"
1¼"

Back

fold

→ *Direction of knitting*
···· *Pick up and knit*
- - - *Seam*
▨ *Knitting*

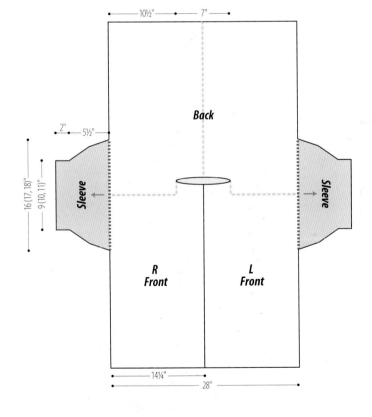

10½"   7"

Back

2"   5½"

16 (17, 18)"
9 (10, 11)"

Sleeve

Sleeve

**R
Front**

**L
Front**

14¼"

28"

PUK

[Pick up and knit a stitch, skip 2 weft threads] to end (page 10). Count stitches and increase or decrease to required number on the next row.

REVERSE STOCKINETTE

Purl RS rows and knit WS rows.

DEC 1

At beginning of WS rows K1, k2tog.
At end of WS rows K2tog, k1.

Summer dress whites

WEAVING

KNITTING

SEWING

STANDARD FIT

S (M, L, 1X)
Shown in SMALL, page 71

A 40 (44, 48, 52)"
38 (42, 46, 50)"
B Maximum length of back
23"; shorten as desired
* C 23 (24, 25, 26)"

12- OR 12.5-dent heddle
15" minimum width
* Width measurements are
given for 12-dent heddle
and will be ½" less for
12.5-dent heddle

2 shuttles

1"

13
12 OR 12.5

12 OR 12.5 warp threads
and 13 weft threads in plain
weave, on the loom

1   4

Medium weight
A 720 (740, 770, 790) yds
6 balls

Super Fine weight
B 370 (390, 420, 450) yds
3 (3, 4, 4) oz

C 130 (130, 140, 145) yds
1 (1, 1, 2) balls

D 250 (270, 290, 310) yds
2 (3, 3, 3) oz

&

Waste yarn

Sewing machine with
zigzag capability

THE WOVEN FABRIC

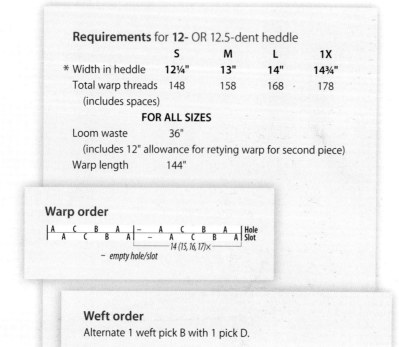

Requirements for **12-** OR 12.5-dent heddle

	S	M	L	1X
* Width in heddle	**12¼"**	**13"**	**14"**	**14¾"**
Total warp threads	148	158	168	178
(includes spaces)				

FOR ALL SIZES
Loom waste   36"
(includes 12" allowance for retying warp for second piece)
Warp length   144"

Warp order

A C B A   —   A C B A   Hole
A C B A   —   A C B A   Slot
     — 14 (15, 16, 17)×
— empty hole/slot

Weft order
Alternate 1 weft pick B with 1 pick D.

WEAVING THE FABRIC

Directions are given for weaving one piece, removing it from the loom, then weaving the other piece.
Warp loom. Wind a shuttle with B and another with D. Following the Weft Order, weave until piece measures 25", end with shuttles at right selvedge. Mark 24 warp threads from left edge (**c**).

SHAPE NECK Weave to marker for front section; wind a butterfly (page 26) with D and weave across remaining 24 warp threads for back neck hem. Work both sections for 1".

Continue to weave front section, leaving 24 warp threads at left edge unwoven, until piece measures 54". Weave ½" with waste yarn. Advance warp and cut between waste section and heddle. Remove fabric from loom and retie warp to front apron. Weave second piece. Weave ½" with waste yarn and remove from loom; zigzag raw edges and back neck as shown.

FINISHING THE FABRIC
Hand wash gently and lay flat to dry.

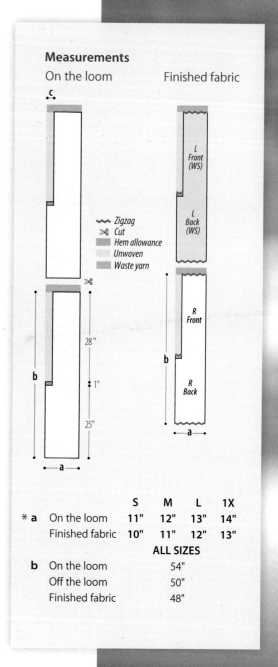

Measurements
On the loom   Finished fabric

~~~ Zigzag
✂ Cut
▨ Hem allowance
☐ Unwoven
▤ Waste yarn

		S	M	L	1X
* **a**	On the loom	11"	12"	13"	14"
	Finished fabric	10"	11"	12"	13"
			ALL SIZES		
b	On the loom		54"		
	Off the loom		50"		
	Finished fabric		48"		

DESIGN CONCEPT

The weaving is done in two panels. The fronts taper to points and hang longer than the back. The neck is shaped on the loom to allow room for the collar, which is knit, as are the sleeves. The whole garment is loose and airy with a nice drape. A little sparkle is provided by tiny sequins in one of the yarns.

A TAHKI YARNS Ripple in color 01 Pearl

B SILK CITY FIBERS Bambu 7 in color 333 Cloud

C S. CHARLES COLLEZIONE Crystal in color 22 Paper Moon

D SILK CITY FIBERS Perle 5/2 Cotton in color 001 Ivory

PUTTING IT ALL TOGETHER

Place right front/back beside left front/back. With D, sew center back seam using Baseball Stitch (page 15). Fold neck hem allowance to WS, turn under edge, then hem (page 15).

SHOULDER DARTS With RS together, fold piece lengthwise 1" above back neck to locate shoulder; stitch darts as shown.

Knit the sleeves (next page). Sew sleeve seams.

BACK HEM With D and beginning at underarm, sew side seams for 8" using Baseball Stitch (leave remainder of seam open until length has been determined).

Mark back length approximately at high hip (19" below back neck on sample garment). Allowing 1" for hem allowance, zigzag and trim away excess fabric. Fold hem allowance to WS, turn under edge, then hem. Complete side seams.

FRONT HEMS Pin or baste to mark angled length from 1" below hemmed back at side seam to 4" below hemmed back at center front. Zigzag and trim as shown; hem as for back.

Knit the collar (next page).

FINISHING THE JACKET

Hand wash gently and lay flat to dry.

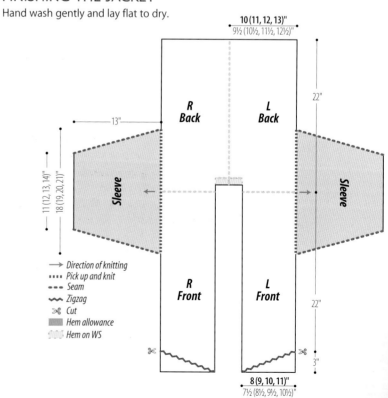

→ Direction of knitting
···· Pick up and knit
- - - Seam
〜〜 Zigzag
✂ Cut
▨ Hem allowance
▨ Hem on WS

PUK

[**Pick up and knit a stitch, skip 2 weft or warp threads**] to end (page 10). Count stitches and increase or decrease to required number on the next row.

STOCKINETTE

Knit RS rows and purl WS rows.

REVERSE STOCKINETTE

Purl RS rows and knit WS rows.

DEC 1

At beginning of RS rows K1, SSK.
At end of RS rows K2tog, k1.

INC 1 EACH SIDE OF RS ROW

K1, R Inc, knit to last stitch, L Inc, k1.

Lifted Increase

R Inc Knit into right loop of stitch in row below stitch on left needle.

L Inc Knit into left loop of stitch 2 rows below stitch on right needle.

4.5mm/US7, 60cm (24") long

10cm/4"
28
18
over garter stitch

&

Sewing needle and thread
Tapestry needle

See Knitting Basics on page 10 for unfamiliar techniques.

KNITTING THE SLEEVES

Measure 9 (9½, 10, 10½)" from shoulder seams and mark side edges. With RS facing and A, pick up and knit (PUK) between markers (page 10). Purl 1 row, adjusting to 81 (86, 90, 95) stitches. Working in Stockinette, Dec 1 each side of next row, [**work 7 rows even; Dec 1 each side of next row**] 4 times, [**work 3 rows even; Dec 1 each side of next row**] 10 times — 51 (56, 60, 65) stitches. Work even until sleeve measures 12", end with a WS row. Knit 2 rows. Work 3 rows Reverse Stockinette. Bind off.

KNITTING THE COLLAR

With RS facing and A, PUK along front edges and back neck. Purl 1 row, adjusting to 254 stitches for length shown. Working in Stockinette, Inc 1 each side of next row, then [**work 3 rows even; Inc 1 each side of next row**] 5 times — 12 stitches increased. Purl 1 row.

Work short rows to shape right front as follows:
Next 2 rows K**70**, W&T, purl to end.
Next 2 rows K1, R Inc, k**60**, W&T, purl to end.
Next 2 rows K**50**, W&T, purl to end.
Next 2 rows K1, R Inc, k**40**, W&T, purl to end,
Next 2 rows K**30**, W&T, purl to end.
Next 2 rows K1, R Inc, k**20**, W&T, purl to end.
Next 2 rows K**10**, W&T, purl to end.
Next row (RS) K1, R Inc, knit to last stitch, hiding wraps, L Inc, k1.

Work short rows to shape left front as follows:
Next 2 rows P**70**, W&T, knit to end.
Next 2 rows P**60**, W&T, knit to last stitch, L Inc, k1.
Next 2 rows P**50**, W&T, knit to end.
Next 2 rows P**40**, W&T, knit to last stitch, L Inc, k1.
Next 2 rows P**30**, W&T, knit to end.
Next 2 rows P**20**, W&T, knit to last stitch, L Inc, k1.
Next 2 rows P**10**, W&T, knit to end.
Next row (WS) Purl all stitches, hiding wraps.
Starting with a purl row, work 3 rows Reverse Stockinette. Bind off.

W&T for short rows

Each short row adds 2 rows of knitting across a section of the work. Since the work is turned before completing a row, stitches must be wrapped at the turn to prevent holes.

 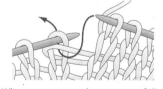

1 With yarn in back, slip next stitch as if to purl. Bring yarn to front of work and slip stitch back to left needle (as shown). Turn work.

2 With yarn in front, slip next stitch as if to purl. Work to end.

3 When you come to the wrap on a following knit row, hide the wrap by knitting it together with the stitch it wraps.

Light & shade jacket

WEAVING

KNITTING

SEWING

S (M, L, 1X)
Shown in SMALL, page 75

A 40 (45, 51, 56)"
39 (42, 50, 55)"

B Maximum length 32";
shorten as desired

* **C** 30¼ (31, 33, 34¼)"

12- OR 12.5-dent heddle
20" minimum width

* Width measurements are
given for 12-dent heddle
and will be ½" less for
12.5-dent heddle

2 shuttles

1"

9

12 OR 12.5

12 OR 12.5 warp threads
and 9 weft threads in plain
weave, on the loom

Light weight

A 1230 (1300, 1360,
1430) yds
11 (12, 12, 13) skeins

B 640 (700, 750, 810) yds
6 (7, 7, 8) skeins

Super Fine weight

C 610 (670, 720, 780) yds
5 (6, 6, 6) oz

Sewing machine with
zigzag capability

Removable stitch markers

THE WOVEN FABRIC: WARPS I AND II, BODY

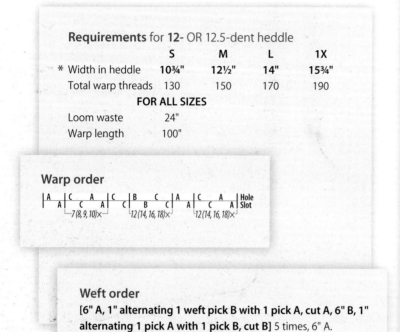

Requirements for **12-** OR 12.5-dent heddle

	S	M	L	1X
* Width in heddle	10¾"	12½"	14"	15¾"
Total warp threads	130	150	170	190
FOR ALL SIZES				
Loom waste	24"			
Warp length	100"			

Warp order

A C A B C A C A   Hole
  A C A C B C A C A Slot
  └7 (8, 9, 10)×┘ └12 (14, 16, 18)×┘ └12 (14, 16, 18)×┘

Weft order

[6" A, 1" alternating 1 weft pick B with 1 pick A, cut A, 6" B, 1" alternating 1 pick A with 1 pick B, cut B] 5 times, 6" A.

WEAVING THE FABRIC: WARPS I AND II

Keep notes while weaving WARP I so you can weave WARP II to match.

Warp loom. Wind a shuttle with A and another with B. Following the Weft Order for Warps I and II, weave until piece measures 37", end with shuttle at right selvedge.

SHAPE NECK Weave across first 84 (100, 118, 134) warp threads (**c**) for front section; wind a butterfly (page 26) with B and weave across remaining warp threads (**d**) for back neck hem. Work both sections for 1". Mark for shoulder. Continue to weave front section, leaving back neck warp threads unwoven, until piece measures 76" (**b**) (38" from shoulder marker). Remove from loom; zigzag raw edges and back neck as shown. Trim off unwoven warp threads. Re-warp loom and weave Warp II to match.

Measurements
On the loom

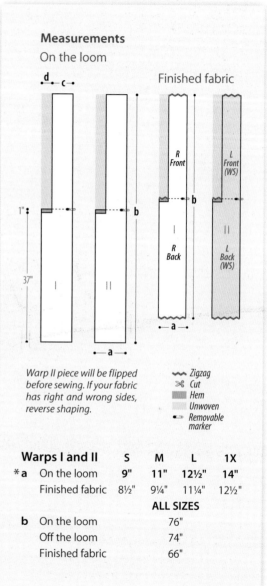

Finished fabric

Warp II piece will be flipped before sewing. If your fabric has right and wrong sides, reverse shaping.

〰 Zigzag
✄ Cut
▨ Hem
▢ Unwoven
•⟶ Removable marker

Warps I and II	S	M	L	1X
* **a** On the loom	9"	11"	12½"	14"
Finished fabric	8½"	9¼"	11¼"	12½"
	ALL SIZES			
b On the loom	76"			
Off the loom	74"			
Finished fabric	66"			

THE WOVEN FABRIC: WARP III, SLEEVES

Requirements

for **12-** OR 12.5-dent heddle

Width in heddle	20"
Total warp threads	**240/248**
Loom waste	24"
Warp length	72"

Warp order

A		C	Hole
	A		
		C	Slot

repeat

Weft order

Weave with B.

Measurements

On the loom	Finished fabric
III	Sleeves
	III

Warp III

a	On the loom	18"
	Finished fabric	17"
b	On the loom	48"
	Off the loom	44"
	Finished fabric	42"

WEAVING THE FABRIC: WARP III

Warp loom. Wind a shuttle with B and weave until piece measures at least 48". Remove from loom; zigzag raw edges.

FINISHING THE FABRIC: WARPS I, II, AND III

Hand wash all pieces in lukewarm water with a little agitation. Use spin cycle or wrap in a towel to remove excess water. Place in dryer on low heat until almost dry. Hang until completely dry.

DESIGN CONCEPT

The jacket is woven using 2 coordinating shades of an ombre yarn, as well as a lightweight bamboo yarn which gives the fabric a lovely feel and drape. The broad warp and weft stripes and the ombre yarns' random color changes create an amorphous plaid pattern. The knit side and sleeve gussets and collar are created with short rows to give the jacket a little flare and an easy fit.

BERROCO LINSEY IN COLORS

A 6566 CAPE POGE   **B** 6565 RIPLEY COVE

C SILK CITY FIBERS BAMBU 7 IN COLOR 160 IRON

PUK

[Pick up and knit a stitch, skip 2 weft or 3 warp threads] to end (page 10). Count stitches and increase or decrease to required number on the next row.

DEC 1

At beginning of row K1, k2tog.
At end of row K2tog, k1.

PUTTING IT ALL TOGETHER
Body

Pin body pieces with RS together; baste and sew back seam with a ¼" seam allowance. Fold hem for back neck to WS, turn under edge, then hem (page 15).

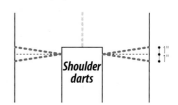

SHOULDER DARTS Fold piece in half lengthwise at shoulder markers. Baste and sew a 1" dart at each shoulder.

Try on and mark finished length. Fold edges to WS, then hem.

Sleeves

Measure 17 (18, 19, 20)" from each cut edge and mark side edges. Zigzag between markers and cut as shown. Fold 1" to WS at each raw edge of sleeve, then hem — 15 (16, 17, 18)". *Note that the woven width is the sleeve length — 17" after washing. You will pick up stitches and knit a 4" cuff along 1 selvedge. For a shorter sleeve, hem to desired length before adding the cuff.*

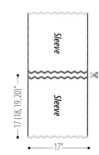

3.75mm/US5,
60cm (24") long
AND spare needle for
3-Needle Bind-Off

10cm/4"
40
21
over garter stitch

Sewing needle
and thread

Tapestry needle

See Knitting Basics on page 10 for unfamiliar techniques.

KNITTING THE SIDE PANELS

Measure 9 (9½, 10, 10½)" from shoulder seams and mark side edges for armholes.

LEFT FRONT With RS facing and A, pick up and knit (PUK) from bottom edge to marker. Knit 4 rows. Purl 1 row. Knit 5 rows. Purl 1 row. Knit 8 rows. ***Begin short rows: Next 2 rows*** Knit to last 15, W&T; knit to end. **[Knit to 15 before last wrap, W&T; knit to end]** 6 times. ***Next row*** Knit all stitches, hiding wraps. Put stitches on spare needle.

LEFT BACK With RS facing and A, PUK the same number of stitches from marker to bottom edge. Knit 4 rows. Purl 1 row. Knit 5 rows. Purl 1 row. Knit 7 rows. Work short rows as for left front **EXCEPT** on WS rows. With RS together, use 3-Needle Bind-Off to join left front to left back (page 11).

Work right front as for left back. Work right back as for left front and join to right front.

KNITTING THE SLEEVE GUSSETS

FIRST GUSSET With RS facing and A, PUK along 1 hemmed edge. Knit 1 row, adjusting to 90 stitches. ***Begin short rows: Next 2 rows*** (RS) Knit to last 22, W&T; knit to end. **[Knit to 12 before last wrap, W&T; knit to end]** 5 times. ***Next row*** Knit all stitches, hiding wraps. Bind off.

SECOND GUSSET With RS facing and A, PUK the same number of stitches along other hemmed edge. Knit 2 rows. Work short rows as for first gusset EXCEPT on WS rows. ***Next row*** Knit all stitches, hiding wraps. Bind off.

KNITTING THE CUFFS

With RS facing and A, PUK along bottom edge of sleeve. Knit 1 row. With B, knit 1 row, then Dec 1 each side of next row. With A, **[knit 5 rows, purl 1 row]** twice. With B, knit 8 rows. With A, knit 1 row, purl 1 row. With B, knit 8 rows. With A, knit 2 rows. With B, knit 2 rows. Bind off.

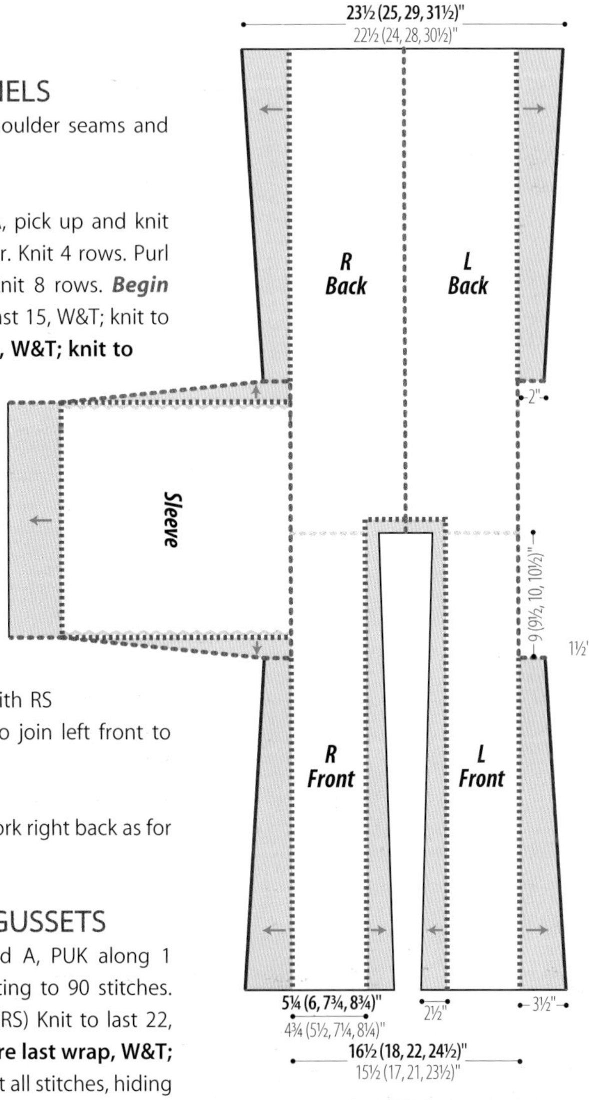

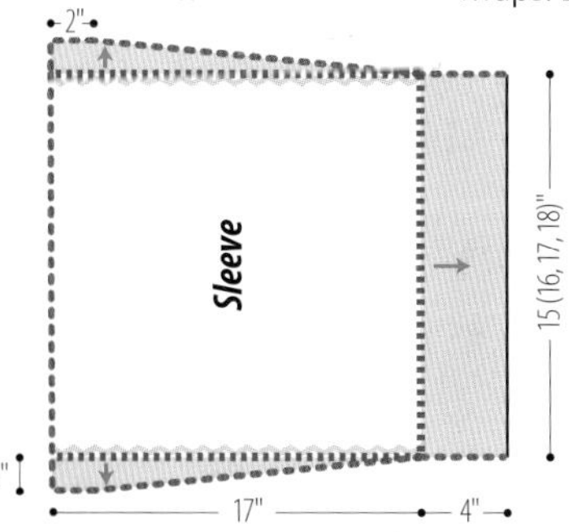

KNITTING THE COLLAR

LEFT SIDE With RS facing, A, and beginning at center of back neck, PUK along back neck hem and left front edge. Knit 1 row. With B, knit 2 rows. Cut B. With A, knit 1 row, purl 1 row, knit 5 rows, purl 1 row, knit 3 rows. ***Begin short rows: Next 2 rows*** (WS) Knit to last 44, W&T; knit to end. **[Knit to 15 before last wrap, W&T; knit to end]** 4 times. ***Next row*** Knit all stitches, hiding wraps. Bind off.

RIGHT SIDE With RS facing, A, and beginning at bottom edge of right front, PUK the same number of stitches along right front edge to center of back neck. Knit 1 row. With B, knit 2 rows. Cut B. With A, knit 1 row, purl 1 row, knit 5 rows, purl 1 row, knit 4 rows. Work short rows as for left side EXCEPT on RS rows. ***Next row*** Knit all stitches, hiding wraps. Bind off.

FINISHING THE JACKET

Sew sleeves into armholes using Baseball Stitch (page 15) and following diagram. Sew sleeve seams. Sew edges of center back collar together.

Diagram labels

23½ (25, 29, 31½)"
22½ (24, 28, 30½)"

R Back

L Back

Sleeve

Sleeve

9 (9½, 10, 10½)"

15 (16, 17, 18)"

2"
2"
1½"
17"
4"

R Front

L Front

→ Direction of knitting
···· Pick up and knit
--- Seam
— 3-needle bind-off
▨ Knitting

5¼ (6, 7¾, 8¾)"
4¾ (5½, 7¼, 8¼)"
2½"
3½"
16½ (18, 22, 24½)"
15½ (17, 21, 23½)"

W&T for short rows

Each short row adds 2 rows of knitting across a section of the work. Since the work is turned before completing a row, stitches must be wrapped at the turn to prevent holes.

1 With yarn in back, slip next stitch as if to purl. Bring yarn to front of work and slip stitch back to left needle (as shown). Turn work.

2 With yarn in front, slip next stitch as if to purl. Work to end.

3 When you come to the wrap on a following knit row, hide the wrap by knitting it together with the stitch it wraps.

Sunshine jacket

LOOSE FIT

6 (8, 10)
Shown in size 10, page 79

A 30 (33, 36)"
Measure around chest at
widest point and add
5 (6, 7)" for ease.
B Maximum length 21";
shorten as desired.
C 18½ (20¾, 23½)"

10-dent heddle
12" minimum width

2 shuttles

10 warp threads and 8 weft
threads in plain weave, on
the loom

Light weight

A 419 (467, 520) yds
5 (6, 6) balls
B 364 (387, 410) yds
5 balls
C 123 (131, 139) yds
2 balls
D 64 (73, 82) yds
1 ball

Waste yarn

Sewing machine with
zigzag capability

THE WOVEN FABRIC

Requirements for 10-dent heddle

	6	8	10
Width in heddle	10¼"	11"	11¾"
Total warp threads	102	110	118
FOR ALL SIZES			
Loom waste	24"		
Warp length	147"		

Warp order

Weft order
Back Alternate 1 weft pick A with 1 pick B throughout.
Fronts: Pocket design [**1 pick A, 1 pick B**] 4 times (pocket hem), [**(2 picks D, 2 picks B) twice, 2 picks D, (1 pick B, 1 pick A) 4 times**] twice, [**2 picks D, 2 picks B**] twice, 2 picks D. Continue alternating 1 pick A with 1 pick B for balance of piece.

WEAVING THE FABRIC

Warp loom. Wind a shuttle each with A, B, and D. Weave, following the Weft Order:

Back Weave until piece measures 55". Weave 1" with waste yarn.

Front *Since the first 12 warp ends at the left edge (d) will not be used again, you may cut them and let them hang off the back of the loom.* Weave the pocket design, then continue as directed until piece measures 31", end with both shuttles at right selvedge.

SHAPE NECK Weave first 72 (76, 80) threads; wind a butterfly (page 26) with A and weave neck hem facing on 18 (22, 26) remaining threads. Work both sections at the same time for 7 more rows (hem facing), then change hem facing butterfly to waste yarn and weave both sections for 3". With waste yarn, weave across all warp ends for 1".
When working neck shaping on second front piece, weave the hem facing, but it is not necessary to weave in waste yarn.

At the end of the weaving, weave a few rows of waste across the entire warp. Remove from loom; zigzag raw edges.

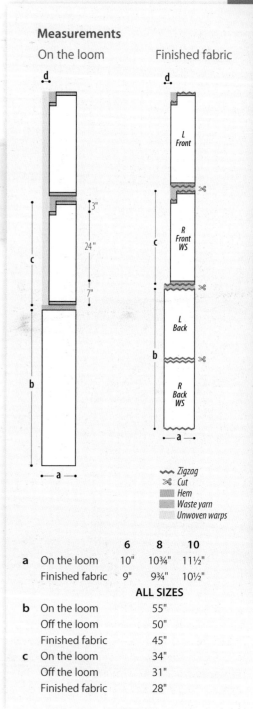

Measurements

On the loom   Finished fabric

		6	8	10
a	On the loom	10"	10¾"	11½"
	Finished fabric	9"	9¾"	10½"
	ALL SIZES			
b	On the loom		55"	
	Off the loom		50"	
	Finished fabric		45"	
c	On the loom		34"	
	Off the loom		31"	
	Finished fabric		28"	

Zigzag
Cut
Hem
Waste yarn
Unwoven warps

DESIGN CONCEPT

The big pockets are created by simply folding up the fabric on the front panels. The neckline is shaped on the loom. Knitting is used for the buttonbands and collar as well as the sleeves — the pieces that would require cutting and shaping if woven. The Fair Isle pattern in the sleeves mimics the woven pattern and ties the design together.

CLASSIC ELITE, JIL EATON COTTONTAIL IN COLORS

A 7532 PLUM

B 7588 BITTERSWEET

C 7585 ORANGINI

D 7535 LIME

FINISHING THE FABRIC

Zigzag and cut the 2 front pieces from the back piece, leaving back as 1 piece. Remove waste. Hand wash in cold water with mild soap. Rinse. Use spin cycle or wrap in a towel to remove excess water. Place in dryer on low heat until almost dry. Lay flat until completely dry. Steam press using a wet towel. Zigzag and cut back piece into 2 equal lengths as shown.

K2, P1 RIB *MULTIPLE OF 3 + 2*
Row 1 (WS) P2, [k1, p2] to end.
Row 2 K2, [p1, k2] to end.
Repeat Rows 1 and 2.

PUK
[Pick up and knit a stitch, skip 2 weft or warp threads] to end (page 10). Count stitches and increase or decrease to required number on the next row.

PUTTING IT ALL TOGETHER

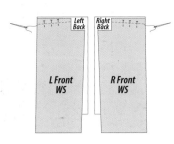

1a With RS together, pin right front and right back shoulders together on the diagonal. Sew seam. Repeat for left front and back.

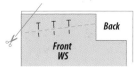

b Clip corner of seam allowance.

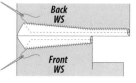

c Turn under raw edges at shoulder and back neck, then hem.

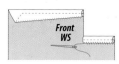

2 Turn under front neck, then hem.

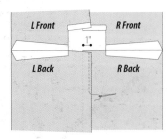

3 Overlap backs; machine stitch, leaving 7" open at hem.

4 Press seams open, using steam.

5 Pin back hem in place. Do not sew; you may need to adjust length.

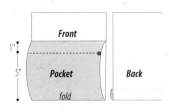

6a Turn RS out and fold up pockets so front length matches back length. Place pin 5" from fold and measure 1" for pocket hem. Zigzag and trim away excess fabric if necessary.

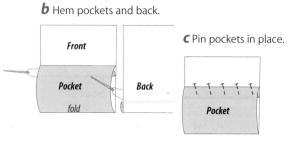

b Hem pockets and back.

c Pin pockets in place.

4mm/US6 and
5mm/US8

10cm/4"
28
20
over stockinette, using
larger needles

&

Sewing needle
and thread
Straight pins
Tapestry needle
Stitch marker
6 22mm (⅞") buttons
1 decorative button for
back (optional)

See Knitting Basics on
page 10 for unfamiliar
techniques.

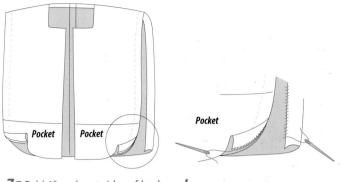

7a Fold 1" under at sides of back and fronts, including double layer of pocket edges, …

b … and sew in place.

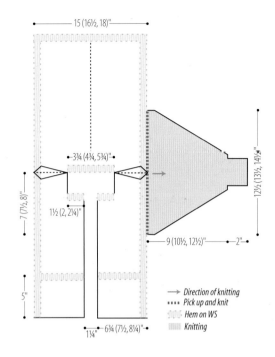

Direction of knitting
Pick up and knit
Hem on WS
Knitting

KNITTING THE SLEEVES

Mark front and back side edges 7 (7½, 8)" down from shoulder seams. With RS facing, larger needles, and A, pick up and knit (PUK) between markers, adjusting to 64 (68, 72) on next row. Purl 1 row. **Next row [K1A, k1B]** to end. **Next row [P1A, p1B]** to end. Repeat last 2 rows once more. **Decrease row** K1, SSK, work to last 3, k2tog, k1. Continue in pattern, working Decrease Row every 4 rows 8 (10, 12) more times, then every 6 rows twice and AT SAME TIME, when sleeve measures 4 (5, 6)", cut B — 42 stitches.

Continue in stockinette with A only until sleeve measures 2" less than desired length to wrist. **Next row** (RS) K2, **[k2tog, k2]** to end — 32 stitches. Change to smaller needles. Work K2, P1 Rib for 2", end with a WS row. Work 3 rows stockinette. Bind off in purl.

KNITTING THE BUTTONBAND

Directions are given for 14 (17½, 21)" length. If your length is different, adjust distance between buttonholes accordingly.
With RS facing, smaller needles, and A, PUK along left front edge, adjusting to a multiple of 3 + 2 on first row. Work K2, P1 Rib for 8 rows. Bind off in pattern.

KNITTING THE BUTTONHOLE BAND

Repeat for left front edge EXCEPT work in K2, P1 Rib for 3 rows. **Next row** (RS) Work 8, **[bind off 2, work until there are 13 stitches on right needle after bind-off]** 3 (4, 5) times, bind off 2, work remaining stitches. **Next row** Work across, casting on 2 above bound-off stitches. Work 3 more rows. Bind off in pattern.

KNITTING THE COLLAR

With RS facing, smaller needles, A, and beginning at buttonhole band edge, PUK 6 in band, PUK along front neck to shoulder, PUK across back neck, PUK along front neck to band, PUK 6 in band, adjusting to a multiple of 3 + 2 on first row. Work in K2, P1 Rib for 8 rows. Starting with a purl row, work 5 rows in stockinette. Bind off.

FINISHING THE JACKET

Block sleeves to finished measurements. Sew sleeve seams using Mattress Stitch (page 15) and side seams using Blind Stitch (page 15).

Sew on buttons. If desired, sew decorative button on back just below collar.

XS (S, M, L, 1X)
Shown in SMALL, page 83

A 37 (41, 45, 49, 53)"
To choose your size,
measure around chest/hips
at widest point and add
6–8" for ease.
B Maximum length 34";
shorten as desired.
C Maximum length
31 (32, 33, 34, 35)"

12- OR 12.5-dent heddle
20" minimum width
* Width measurements are
given for 12-dent heddle
and will be ½" less for
12.5-dent heddle.

2 shuttles

1"

12

12 OR 12.5

12 OR 12.5 warp threads
and 12 weft threads in plain
weave, on the loom

1 3 4

Light weight
A 1000 (1110, 1170, 1240,
1300) yds
8 (9, 10, 10, 11) skeins

D 200 (200, 220, 240,
260) yds
2 (2, 3, 3, 3) skeins

Medium weight
B 90 yds
1 skein
C 95 yds
1 skein

Super Fine weight
E 1240 (1340, 1410, 1420,
1450) yds
10 (11, 11, 11, 11) oz

&

Sewing machine with
zigzag capability

Big pockets jacket

THE WOVEN FABRIC: WARP I, BACK PANELS

Requirements for **12-** OR 12.5-dent heddle

	XS	S	M	L	1X
* Width in heddle	13½"	14½"	15½"	16½"	17½"
Total warp threads	164	176	188	200	212
FOR ALL SIZES					
Loom waste	24"				
Warp length	110"				

Warp order for Warps I and II

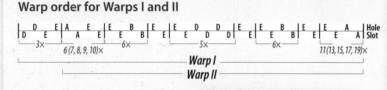

**Weft order
for Warps I, II, and III**
Alternate 1 weft pick A with
1 pick E.

THE WOVEN FABRIC: WARP II, FRONT PANELS

Requirements for **12-** OR 12.5-dent heddle

	XS	S	M	L	1X
* Width in heddle	12½"	13½"	14½"	15½"	16½"
Total warp threads	152	164	176	188	200
FOR ALL SIZES					
Loom waste	24"				
Warp length	124"				

WEAVING THE FABRIC: WARPS I, II, AND III

Warp loom. Wind a shuttle with A and another with E. Following the Weft Order for Warps I, II, or III, weave until piece measures at least 86" for Warp I, at least 100" for Warp II, or at least 54" for Warp III. Remove from loom; zigzag raw edges.

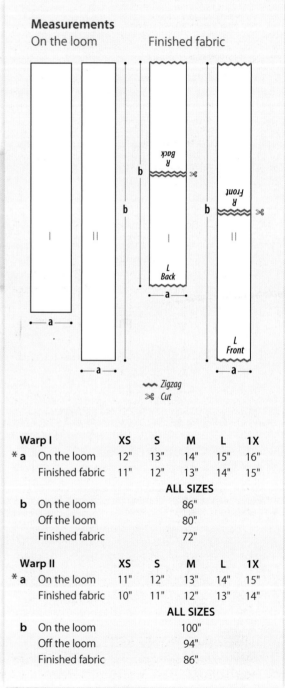

Measurements
On the loom   Finished fabric

Zigzag
Cut

Warp I		XS	S	M	L	1X
* **a**	On the loom	12"	13"	14"	15"	16"
	Finished fabric	11"	12"	13"	14"	15"
	ALL SIZES					
b	On the loom	86"				
	Off the loom	80"				
	Finished fabric	72"				

Warp II		XS	S	M	L	1X
* **a**	On the loom	11"	12"	13"	14"	15"
	Finished fabric	10"	11"	12"	13"	14"
	ALL SIZES					
b	On the loom	100"				
	Off the loom	94"				
	Finished fabric	86"				

THE WOVEN FABRIC: WARP III, SLEEVES

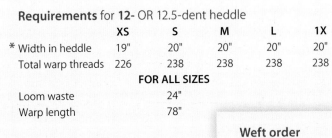

Requirements for **12-** OR **12.5-dent** heddle

	XS	S	M	L	1X
* Width in heddle	19"	20"	20"	20"	20"
Total warp threads	226	238	238	238	238

	FOR ALL SIZES
Loom waste	24"
Warp length	78"

Weft order
See Warps I and II.

Warp order

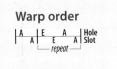

A		E		A	Hole
	A		E		A	Slot

repeat

Measurements

On the loom   Finished fabric

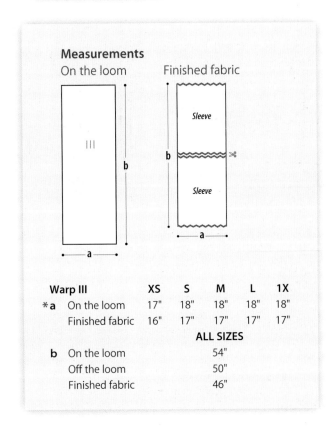

Warp III	XS	S	M	L	1X
*a On the loom	17"	18"	18"	18"	18"
Finished fabric	16"	17"	17"	17"	17"

	ALL SIZES
b On the loom	54"
Off the loom	50"
Finished fabric	46"

FINISHING THE FABRIC

Hand wash. Use spin cycle or wrap in a towel to remove excess water. Place in dryer on low heat for about 10 minutes. Hang until completely dry. Zigzag and cut each piece into 2 equal lengths as shown.

DESIGN CONCEPT

The jacket's straight panels can be easily adjusted for length and width. Big pockets are created by simply folding up the fabric on the front panels and the V-neck is shaped by folding back the fabric and clipping off the corner. The simple, bold stripe pattern is both striking and flattering. Knitting is used for the buttonbands and collar as well as to expand the width of the upper sleeves. Pleating the cuff creates a graceful, flowing sleeve.

A BERROCO FUJI IN COLOR 9238 STORMCLOUD

BERROCO CAPTIVA IN COLORS

B 5543 PATINA   **C** 5534 NOTTE

D BERROCO LAGO IN COLOR 8440 PASSION FLOWER

E SILK CITY FIBERS BAMBU 7 IN COLOR 360 ONYX

PUK
[Pick up and knit a stitch, skip 2 warp or weft threads] to end (page 10). Count stitches and increase or decrease to required number on the next row.

K2, P1, RIB
MULTIPLE OF 3 + 2
Row 1 (RS) K2, **[p1, k2]** to end.
Row 2 P2, **[k1, p2]** to end.
Repeat Rows 1 and 2.

3.5mm/US4, 60cm (24") or longer
AND
spare needle for
3-Needle Bind-Off

10cm/4"

32

24

24 stitches and 32 rows to 10cm/4" over K2, P1 Rib

&

Sewing needle and thread

2 large snaps

10 25mm (1") buttons

Tapestry needle

Safety pins

See Knitting Basics on page 10 for unfamiliar techniques.

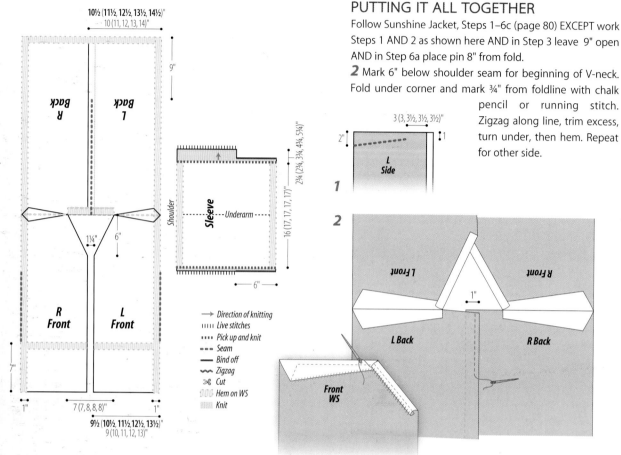

PUTTING IT ALL TOGETHER
Follow Sunshine Jacket, Steps 1–6c (page 80) EXCEPT work Steps 1 AND 2 as shown here AND in Step 3 leave 9" open AND in Step 6a place pin 8" from fold.

2 Mark 6" below shoulder seam for beginning of V-neck. Fold under corner and mark ¾" from foldline with chalk pencil or running stitch. Zigzag along line, trim excess, turn under, then hem. Repeat for other side.

KNITTING THE BUTTONBAND
With RS facing and C, pick up and knit (PUK) along left front edge, from beginning of neck shaping to bottom edge, working through both layers at pockets. Knit 1 row, adjusting to a multiple of 3 + 2. Cut C. With A, work K2, P1 Rib for 8 rows. Cut A. With C, work 1 row in rib. Bind off in pattern.

KNITTING THE BUTTONHOLE BAND
Directions are given for 28" length. If your length is different, adjust distance between buttonholes accordingly.
With RS facing and C, PUK along right front edge, from bottom edge to beginning of neck shaping. Knit 1 row, adjusting to a multiple of 3 + 2. Cut C. With A, work in K2, P1 Rib for 3 rows. **Next row** (WS) Work 3, **[bind off 2, work until there are 16 stitches on right needle after bind-off]** 7 times, bind off 2, work remaining stitches. **Next row** Work across, casting on 2 above bound-off stitches. Work 3 more rows in rib. Cut A. With C, work 1 row in rib. Bind off in pattern.

KNITTING THE COLLAR
With RS facing and C, PUK 7 along top of buttonhole band, PUK around neck, and PUK 7 along top of buttonband. Knit 1 row. Do not cut. With D, work 3 rows stockinette. Slide stitches to other end of circular needle. With C, knit 1 row. Do not cut. With D, work 3 rows stockinette. Cut D. Slide stitches to other end of needle. With C, purl 3 rows. Starting with a knit row, work 6 rows stockinette. Bind off. Cut, leaving long tail for sewing. Fold collar to inside at purl ridge and sew in place.

FINISHING THE JACKET
Sew on buttons. Sew a button to each pocket. Sew snap to each pocket behind button.

Make sleeves and cuffs (next page). With tapestry needle and A, sew sleeves to body using Blind Stitch (page 15), centering knit panel at shoulder seam. Sew side seams using Blind Stitch, leaving 7" open at bottom.

Sleeves

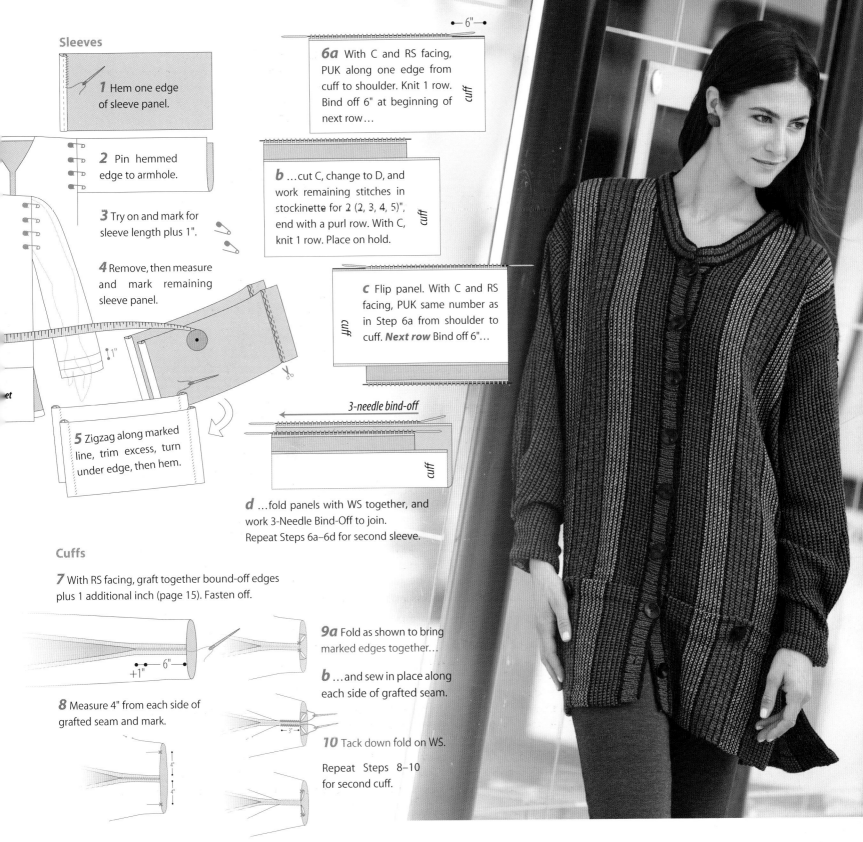

1 Hem one edge of sleeve panel.

2 Pin hemmed edge to armhole.

3 Try on and mark for sleeve length plus 1".

4 Remove, then measure and mark remaining sleeve panel.

1"

5 Zigzag along marked line, trim excess, turn under edge, then hem.

6"

6a With C and RS facing, PUK along one edge from cuff to shoulder. Knit 1 row. Bind off 6" at beginning of next row…

cuff

b …cut C, change to D, and work remaining stitches in stockinette for 2 (2, 3, 4, 5)", end with a purl row. With C, knit 1 row. Place on hold.

cuff

c Flip panel. With C and RS facing, PUK same number as in Step 6a from shoulder to cuff. **Next row** Bind off 6"…

cuff

3-needle bind-off

cuff

d …fold panels with WS together, and work 3-Needle Bind-Off to join. Repeat Steps 6a–6d for second sleeve.

Cuffs

7 With RS facing, graft together bound-off edges plus 1 additional inch (page 15). Fasten off.

+1" 6"

8 Measure 4" from each side of grafted seam and mark.

4"
4"

9a Fold as shown to bring marked edges together…

b …and sew in place along each side of grafted seam.

10 Tack down fold on WS.

Repeat Steps 8–10 for second cuff.

85

Sorbet jacket

WEAVING

SEWING

LOOSE FIT

S (M, L, 1X)
Shown in SMALL, page 87

A 25 (27, 29, 31)" across back at underarm
B Length from shoulder fold to hem 21". On the body, the jacket sits back on the shoulders and the back length is 24".
C 31½ (33, 34, 35)"

10-dent heddle
20" minimum width

2 shuttles

20 warp threads and 20 weft threads in plain weave, on the loom (2 per slot/hole in 10-dent heddle) (2 picks per shed)

Super Fine weight

A 2350 (2410, 2480, 2540) yds
12 (12, 13, 13) balls

B 1050 (1090, 1120, 1160) yds
6 balls

C 725 (750, 780, 810) yds
4 balls

Sewing machine with zigzag capability

Sewing needle and thread

¼ yd lightweight trim fabric (Silkessence, 100% polyester, in color Biking Red)

¼ yd iron-on interfacing

THE WOVEN FABRIC: WARP I, BODY PANELS

Requirements for 10-dent heddle

	S	M	L	1X
Width in heddle	12"	13"	14"	15"
Working warp threads	120	130	140	150
FOR ALL SIZES				
Loom waste	24"			
Warp length	131"			

Warp order

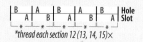

*thread each section 12 (13, 14, 15)×

A and B remain doubled in the warp.

Example: When threading the first 2 sections of the Warp Order, work as follows (reading from right to left):

[Pull loop A through slot, loop B through hole] 12 (13, 14, 15) times.

[Pull loop B through slot, loop A through hole] 12 (13, 14, 15) times.

After winding onto the back beam, it is not necessary to cut the loops; the doubled threads remain in each slot and hole.

Weft order

Alternate 1 double weft pick of A with 1 double pick of C.

To weave a double pick Weave 1 weft pick, beat lightly, and then, without changing sheds, wrap the weft around the last warp thread and bring the shuttle back through the same shed, weaving another pick with the same weft. Beat and change sheds. This keeps the 2 weft threads lying flat and not twisted.

WEAVING THE FABRIC: WARP I (II)

Warp loom. Wind a shuttle with A and another with C. Following the Weft Order for Warp I (II), weave until piece measures at least 104" (at least 40", end with 6 double picks A). Remove from loom; zigzag raw edges. Zigzag and cut into 2 equal lengths as shown.

Measurements

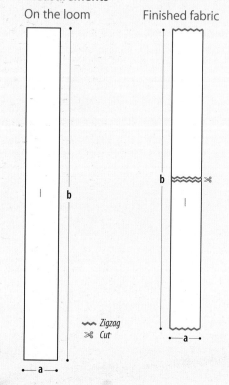

On the loom   Finished fabric

〜〜 Zigzag
✂ Cut

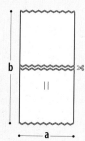

Warp I		S	M	L	1X
a	On the loom	11"	12"	13"	14"
	Finished fabric	10¼"	11¼"	12¼"	13¼"
	ALL SIZES				
b	On the loom	107"			
	Off the loom	100"			
	Finished fabric	96"			
Warp II					
a	On the loom	19"			
	Finished fabric	18"			
b	On the loom	40"			
	Off the loom	38"			
	Finished fabric	36"			

DESIGN CONCEPT

I learned a lesson in drape after weaving 2 straight panels and hanging them on my dress form: They want to cross over each other. The front panels fold back on themselves, which is fine, but I wasn't happy with the back. I added a center back panel and 2 squarish panels to fill in the sides. What resulted was a jacket with a very au courant flair and drape.

The log cabin weave, alternating a space-dyed yarn with a solid color in the warp, created an interesting fabric and, because the design called for 4 separate warps, I was able to vary the warp drafts to create a patchwork effect.

THE WOVEN FABRIC: WARP II, SLEEVES

Requirements
for 10-dent heddle

Width in heddle	20"
Working warp threads	199
Loom waste	24"
Warp length	64"

Weft order
6 double weft picks A, [**1 double pick C, 1 double pick A**] twice, 2 double picks C.

Warp order

A A A B B A A A Hole
A B B A A A B B A Slot
5x 5x 5x 5x 5x 5x 5x
4x

A and B remain doubled in the warp.

CRYSTAL PALACE YARNS Panda Silk in colors

A 3011 Sangria

B 4006 Plum Tones

C 3006 Berry Smoothie

THE WOVEN FABRIC: WARP III, SIDE INSERTS

Requirements
for 10-dent heddle

Width in heddle	16"
Working warp threads	160
Loom waste	24"
Warp length	64"

Warp order

B		A		B	Hole
	A		B		Slot

40×   40×

A and B remain doubled in the warp.

Weft order
[Alternate 1 double weft pick A with 1 double pick C for 10", end 1 double pick A] 4 times.

THE WOVEN FABRIC: WARP IV, BACK INSERT

Requirements
for 10-dent heddle

Width in heddle	8"
Working warp threads	79
Loom waste	24"
Warp length	50"

Warp order

	B	A	B		Hole
A		A		A	Slot

17×   5×   17×

A and B remain doubled in the warp.

Weft order
[1 double weft pick A, 1 double pick C] 5 times, [1 double pick C, 1 double pick A] 5 times.

WEAVING THE FABRIC: WARP III (IV)

Warp loom. Wind a shuttle with A and another with C. Following the Weft Order for Warp III (IV), weave until piece measures at least 40" (26"). Remove from loom; zigzag raw edges. Zigzag and cut Warp III into 2 equal lengths as shown (between second and third repeat of Weft Order).

FINISHING THE FABRIC

Hand wash and dry all pieces. Steam press. Roll top edge of back insert to RS, then hem.

Measurements

On the loom   Finished fabric

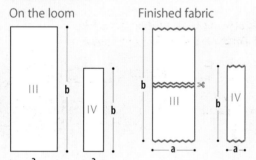

Warp III

a	On the loom	14½"
	Finished fabric	14"
b	On the loom	40"
	Off the loom	38"
	Finished fabric	36"

Warp IV

a	On the loom	7"
	Finished fabric	6"
b	On the loom	26"
	Off the loom	25"
	Finished fabric	24"

PUTTING IT ALL TOGETHER

EXCEPT in Step 7, all hems are rolled to the RS.

1 Seam sleeves Fold one piece of Warp II in half with WS and raw edges together, matching the patterns on each side of fold. Measure 9 (9½, 10, 10½)" from fold, leaving 1" seam allowance; pin and machine stitch seam.
FLAT-FELLED SEAM (page 15) Trim top seam allowance to ½". Fold bottom seam allowance over top seam allowance, turn under edge, then hem on RS.
Repeat for other sleeve.

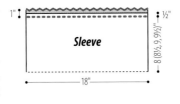

Sleeve
1"
½"
8 (8½, 9, 9½)"
18"

〜〜 Zigzag
- - - Seam
〰〰 Hem on RS

2 Join sleeves to body panels Look at Warp 1 pieces and note that the pattern reverses when you turn the fabric over. Decide which side is the RS and mark both pieces. Fold one piece in half at the shoulder with RS together. Turn sleeve inside out and pin in place, centering top of sleeve at shoulder fold. Sew using Baseball Stitch (page 15). Repeat for other panel.

3 Add side inserts Centering the pattern and allowing 1" seam allowances, mark side inserts to length of front and back side edges. Fold the top raw edge of one piece to the RS (**x**) and pin in place. Pin **x** to back panel and pin adjoining selvedge (**y**) to the front panel; fold under edge of **x**, then hem. From WS, sew **x** to back using Blind Stitch (page 15) and sew **y** to front using Baseball Stitch. Repeat for other insert.

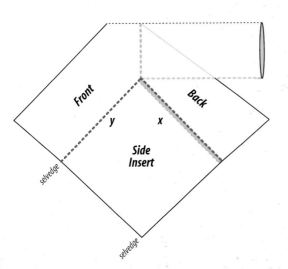

Front
Back
y   x
Side Insert
selvedge
selvedge

4 Trim body panels

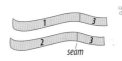
seam

a Tear or cut trim fabric into 3 strips 2½" by width of fabric.

b Cut pieces from 1 strip to lengthen the other strips to 44" each.

c Cut 2 strips of iron-on interfacing 2" by 44".

d Center interfacing on fabric, pin, and iron in place.

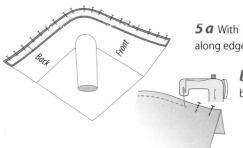
Back   Front

5 a With RS together, pin and sew a strip of trim along edge of half of jacket, placing trim join at back.

b With woven fabric on top, machine stitch between second and third warp threads.

c Press seams toward the trim.

6 a With WS of woven fabric and trim facing, fold cut edge of trim at edge of interfacing and press.

b Fold pressed edge to WS to align with machine stitching and sew to woven fabric using Blind Stitch.

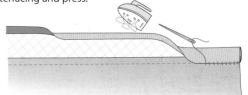

7 a Mark center of back insert and pin in place as shown in diagram: 1½" below shoulder and 2½ (2¾, 3, 3)" from edge of trim. Sew edge of trim to back insert using Blind Stitch.

b On WS, sew side edges of back insert to jacket. Turn bottom edge of jacket to WS, then hem. Press all hems and seams flat.

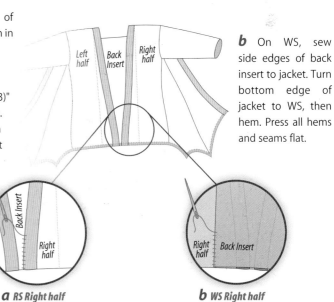
Left half   Back Insert   Right half
Back Insert   Right half
Right half   Back Insert
a RS Right half   **b** WS Right half

Be bold jacket

WEAVING

SEWING

LOOSE FIT

S (M, L, 1X)
Shown in MEDIUM, page 91

A 40 (44, 48, 52)"
B 25 (26, 27½, 29)"
Maximum length 29";
shorten as desired.
C 31 (32, 33, 34)"

10-dent heddle
20" minimum width

2 shuttles

10 warp threads
and 10 weft threads in plain
weave, on the loom

Medium weight

A 1590 (1710, 1850,
1960) yds
8 (8, 9, 9) skeins

B 430 (430, 440, 440) yds
2 skeins

C 130 (130, 130, 130) yds
2 skeins

Sewing machine with
zigzag capability

Sewing needle and thread

³/8" twill tape
(two 9-foot rolls)

Tapestry needle

Straight pins

THE WOVEN FABRIC: WARP I, BACK

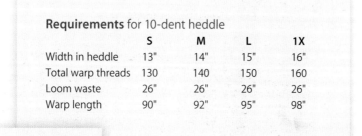

Requirements for 10-dent heddle

	S	M	L	1X
Width in heddle	13"	14"	15"	16"
Total warp threads	130	140	150	160
Loom waste	26"	26"	26"	26"
Warp length	90"	92"	95"	98"

Warp order

A	Hole
A	Slot

65 (70, 75, 80)×

Weft order

LEFT BACK **[8 weft picks B, 10 picks A]** 5 times, 8 picks B. Weave remaining rows with A.

RIGHT BACK Weave with A until armhole measures 3", end with shuttle at right edge. Work 36-row B rectangle as follows: Starting at left edge, weave B over 46 threads. From right edge, weave A over remaining threads, bringing shuttle out in same space as B shuttle. Change shed. Bring both colors back around the same warp thread (see Dovetail Join, page 27).

WEAVING THE FABRIC: WARP I

Warp loom. Wind a shuttle with A and another with B. Following the Weft Order for Warp I, Left Back, weave until piece measures 20 (21, 22, 23)".

SHAPE ARMHOLES With a separate piece of A, weave 1" hem over 32 threads (**c**) from the left edge, then weave shaded section with waste yarn and AT THE SAME TIME, with a separate shuttle, continue to weave to shoulder for 12 (12, 12½, 13)".

Weave waste yarn across entire width for 1" until warp threads are once again evenly spaced. Weave second piece following Warp Order for Right Back and shaping armhole at right edge. It is not necessary to weave in waste for the armhole. Remove from loom; zigzag and cut as shown.

WEAVING THE FABRIC: WARP II

Warp loom. Wind a shuttle with A and another with B. Following the Weft Order for Warp II, weave until piece measures 20 (21, 22, 23)". Shape armhole as for Right Back until armhole measures 11½ (11½, 12, 12½)".

Weave ½" without joining colors A and B. Continue to weave B section for 4", weaving waste yarn across all other warp threads. Weave waste yarn across entire width for 1". Weave second piece to match, without weaving in waste. Note that the second piece will be flipped over when constructing the garment. Remove from loom; zigzag and cut apart as shown.

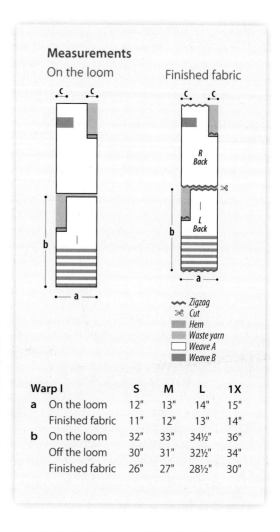

Measurements

On the loom   Finished fabric

R Back

L Back

b   *b*

a   *a*

〰〰 *Zigzag*
✂ *Cut*
▦ *Hem*
▨ *Waste yarn*
☐ *Weave A*
▩ *Weave B*

Warp I		S	M	L	1X
a	On the loom	12"	13"	14"	15"
	Finished fabric	11"	12"	13"	14"
b	On the loom	32"	33"	34½"	36"
	Off the loom	30"	31"	32½"	34"
	Finished fabric	26"	27"	28½"	30"

THE WOVEN FABRIC: WARP II, FRONT

Requirements for 10-dent heddle

	S	M	L	1X
Width in heddle	16"	17"	18"	19"
Total warp threads	160	170	180	190
Loom waste	26"	26"	26"	26"
Warp length	98"	100"	104"	106"

Warp order

C	B	A	Hole
C	B	A	Slot

15×

50 (55, 60, 65)×

Weft order

With B, weave from left across 60 B/C warp threads; with A, weave from right across 100 (110, 120, 130) A warp threads, joining colors using Dovetail Join.

Measurements

On the loom   Finished fabric

c   c

|| ||

                              R
                              Front
                              WS

b   b

|| L
                              Front

a   a

Warp II

		S	M	L	1X
a	On the loom	15"	16"	17"	18"
	Finished fabric	13½"	14½"	15½"	16½"
b	On the loom	32"	33"	34½"	36"
	Off the loom	30"	31"	32½"	34"
	Finished fabric	26"	27"	28½"	30"

DESIGN CONCEPT

The wool yarn I used fulled nicely for a soft, cozy jacket, but this style would also be lovely in a silky fabric. The armholes are shaped on the loom. The collar is woven as part of the front panels, using a tapestry join to connect the two colors. The square in the back is created using the same tapestry join. To achieve a sleeve wide enough to fit the armhole on a 20" loom, the sleeves are woven from seam edge to seam edge (see Sleeve Challenge, page 17). Sleeve shaping is achieved by folding and stitching the bottom edge. The cuff is a separate piece, added for extra length.

CASCADE YARNS CASCADE 220 IN COLORS

A 9484 STRATOSPHERE

B 8555 BLACK

C BERROCO CAPTIVA IN COLOR 5534 NOTTE

THE WOVEN FABRIC: WARP III, SLEEVES

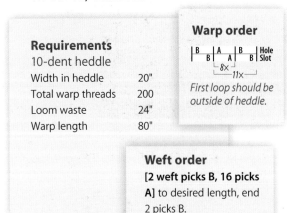

Requirements
10-dent heddle

Width in heddle	20"
Total warp threads	200
Loom waste	24"
Warp length	80"

Warp order

B | B | A | B | Hole
B | A | B | Slot
8×
11×

First loop should be outside of heddle.

Weft order
[2 weft picks B, 16 picks A] to desired length, end 2 picks B.

THE WOVEN FABRIC: WARP IV, CUFFS

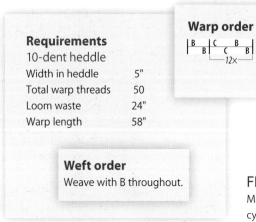

Requirements
10-dent heddle

Width in heddle	5"
Total warp threads	50
Loom waste	24"
Warp length	58"

Warp order

B | C | B | Hole
B | C | B | Slot
12×

Weft order
Weave with B throughout.

WEAVING THE FABRIC: WARP III (IV)

Warp loom. Wind a shuttle with A and another with B. Weave, following the Weft Order for Warp III (IV). Remove from loom; zigzag and cut into 2 equal lengths as shown.

FINISHING THE FABRIC

Machine wash all pieces in warm water, gentle cycle, and mild detergent; use a few drops of fabric softener in final rinse. The goal is a soft, fulled fabric with 12 warp threads and 12 weft threads per inch. Re-wash if necessary. Lay flat to dry.

Measurements

On the loom   Finished fabric

III   IV   b
b   b   IV
b
a   a

~~~ Zigzag
✂ Cut

Warp III
a	On the loom	18½"
	Finished fabric	17"
b	On the loom	56"
	Off the loom	50"
	Finished fabric	46"

Warp IV
a	On the loom	4¾"
	Finished fabric	4½"
b	On the loom	34"
	Off the loom	30"
	Finished fabric	28"

PUTTING IT ALL TOGETHER

1a With RS together, pin right back and left back together and measure ½" from side seam allowance toward center for desired width.

b Machine stitch at desired width and trim corners.

c Press seam open, using steam.

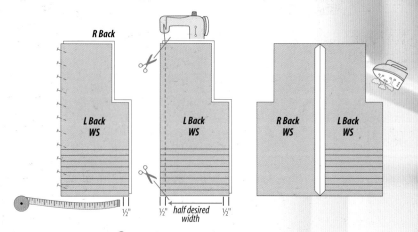

R Back · L Back WS · L Back WS · R Back WS · L Back WS

½" ½" half desired width ½"

2 Join fronts to back at shoulders with diagonal seams.

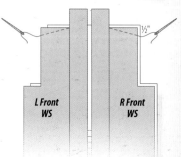

L Front WS   R Front WS

3 Machine stitch side seams and trim corners. Press seams open.

4 Machine stitch twill tape (pink areas in drawing above) to raw edges of shoulders, back neck, and underarm hems. Hand sew twill tape to back hem.

5a With B, sew edge of collar piece to back of neck using Baseball Stitch (page 15). *Collar piece extends beyond center back seam.* Repeat for other collar piece.
b Pin WS of collar together and machine stitch, aligning with center back seam of jacket.

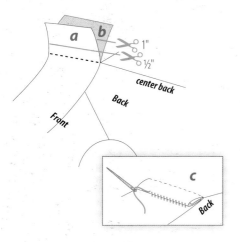

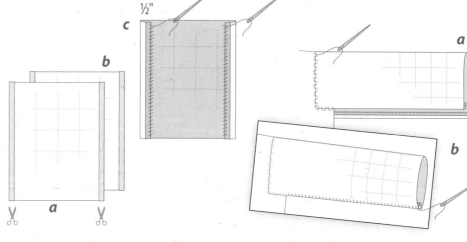

6 Make a flat-felled seam:

   a Trim one collar seam allowance to ½".

   b Trim second seam allowance to 1".

   c Fold longer seam allowance over shorter, tuck raw edge under, then sew in place.

7a Cut sleeves to 19 (19, 20, 21)", centering a black stripe.

   b Machine stitch twill tape to raw edges.

   c Fold under ½", then sew to WS of sleeve. *Twill-taped edges will become underarm seam; selvedges are joined to body and cuff.*

8a Pin sleeve into armhole, centering stripe at shoulder. With B, set in sleeves using Baseball Stitch.

   b Sew underarm seams using Blind Stitch (page 15).

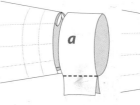
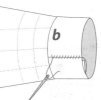

10a Pin WS of cuff together and machine stitch, matching circumference of bottom of sleeve. Attach to sleeve, aligning cuff seam with sleeve seam.

   b Finish with a flat-felled seam as in Step 6.

9 Pleat sleeves at cuff: fold so second stripes from center on each side meet. Sew along length of 2 blocks, attaching to center stripe on bottom layer as well.

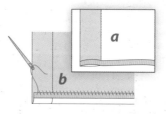

11a Fold front bands back onto themselves at hem, then pin in place.

   b Try on and mark hem; note that front hem may be shorter than back. Trim, add twill tape, then sew hem.

12 Steam garment; flatten all seams and hems.

VESTS

Field of pansies

THE WOVEN FABRIC

WEAVING

S (M, L, 1X, 2X)
Shown in MEDIUM, page 97
A 12 (14, 16, 17, 19)" across
back at shoulders
B 18"

12- OR 12.5-dent heddle
20"minimum width

2 shuttles

12 OR 12.5

12 OR 12.5 warp threads
and 12 weft threads in plain
weave, on the loom

Light weight
A 520 (570, 630, 680,
750) yds
3 skeins

Super Fine weight
B 390 (430, 470, 510,
550) yds
3 (4, 4, 4, 5) oz

Sewing machine with
zigzag capability

Sewing needle and thread

Tapestry needle

Crochet hook 3.5mm/E-4

Requirements for 12- OR 12.5-dent heddle

FOR ALL SIZES

Width in heddle	20"				
Total warp threads	**240**/248				
Loom waste	24"				
	S	**M**	**L**	**1X**	**2X**
Warp length	76"	82"	88"	94"	100"

Warp order

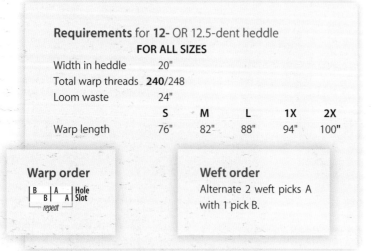

Weft order

Alternate 2 weft picks A
with 1 pick B.

WEAVING THE FABRIC

Warp loom. Wind a shuttle with A and another with B. Following the Weft Order, weave until piece measures 15 (17, 19, 20½, 22½)" (**c**), end with both shuttles at left edge.

SHAPE ARMHOLES Weave across 10" (**f**); with another shuttle, weave across remaining warp threads (**g**) for armhole hem allowance. Work both sections simultaneously for 1", then weave shaded section (**g**) with waste yarn for 2 (2, 2, 3, 3)" (**d**). Weave another 1" hem with A, then continue to weave across all warp threads for 14 (16, 18, 19, 21)" (**e**) to second armhole and repeat shaping.

Weave 15 (17, 19, 20½, 22½)" (**c**). Remove from loom. Zigzag as shown; do **not** cut and remove waste yarn until after piece is washed and dried.

FINISHING THE FABRIC

Wash and dry. Remove waste yarn. Steam press.

Measurements

On the loom   Finished fabric

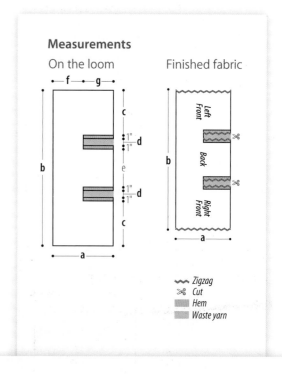

〰〰 Zigzag
✂ Cut
▨ Hem
▨ Waste yarn

	ALL SIZES				
a On the loom			19"		
Finished fabric			18"		
	S	**M**	**L**	**1X**	**2X**
b On the loom	52"	58"	64"	70"	76"
Off the loom	49"	55"	61"	67"	73"
Finished fabric	46"	52"	58"	64"	70"

DESIGN CONCEPT

The shape of this garment is a rectangle with shaped-out armholes. Each front is almost as wide as the back, creating cascading front panels that drape longer than the back. The weaving is done in 1 piece, working from front edge to front edge. Thus, the length of the garment is limited by the width of your loom. To make it longer, you could add a knit or woven border as I did in Desert Varnish Vest (page 98). Field of Pansies was woven with a space-dyed yarn for both warp and weft, which created an interesting plaid-like pattern.

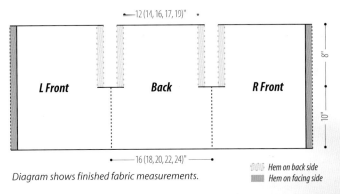

12 (14, 16, 17, 19)"

L Front

Back

R Front

8"

10"

16 (18, 20, 22, 24)"

Diagram shows finished fabric measurements.

Hem on back side
Hem on facing side

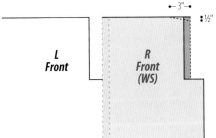

3"

½"

L Front

R Front (WS)

PUTTING IT ALL TOGETHER

Sew shoulder seams on a diagonal as shown. Fold armhole hem allowance to WS, turn under edge, then hem to body. Steam. Try on and adjust width of front panel as desired, fold to RS, turn under edge, then hem.

CROCHET EDGING

With RS facing, crochet hook, and A, work a row of single crochet across selvedges at bottom of vest and at center fronts and neck (page 10).

Place a wet towel on piece and steam flat.

A FIESTA BALLET IN COLOR 155 PANSIES

B SILK CITY FIBERS BAMBU 7 IN COLOR 229 FORGET ME NOT

Desert varnish

A

B

LOOSE FIT

S (M, L, 1X, 2X)
Shown in MEDIUM, page 99

A 12 (14, 16, 17, 19)"
across back at shoulders
B 20½"

12- OR 12.5-dent heddle
20" minimum width

3 shuttles

Tapestry beater
OR kitchen fork

1"

14

12 OR 12.5

12 OR 12.5 warp threads
and 14 weft threads, in
plain weave, on the loom

2 5

Fine weight
A 870 (940, 1020, 1100,
1150) yds
5 (6, 6, 7, 7) skeins

B 160 (170, 200, 220,
240) yds
1 (1, 2, 2, 2) skeins

C 40 (50, 50, 60, 70) yds
1 skein

Bulky weight
D 15 (20, 20, 20, 25) yds
1 skein

&

Sewing machine with
zigzag capability

Sewing needle
and thread

Tapestry needle

THE WOVEN FABRIC: WARP I

Requirements for **12**- OR **12.5**-dent heddle

FOR ALL SIZES

Width in heddle	20"				
Total warp threads	**240**/250				
Loom waste	24"				
	S	M	L	1X	2X
Warp length	76"	82"	88"	94"	100"

Warp order

A	Hole
A	Slot

repeat

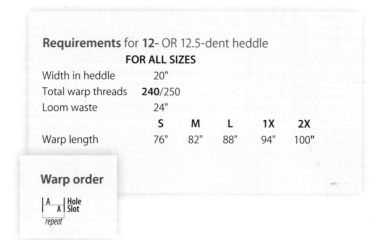

Measurements

On the loom   Finished fabric

Left Front

Back

Right Front

〰 *Zigzag*
✂ *Cut*
▓ *Hem*
▒ *Waste yarn*

ALL SIZES

	Warp I	Warp II
a On the loom	19"	2¾"
Finished fabric	18"	2½"

Warp I and II	XS	S	M	L	1X
b On the loom	52"	58"	64"	70"	76"
Off the loom	49"	55"	61"	67"	73"
Finished fabric	46"	52"	58"	64"	70"

WEAVING THE FABRIC: WARP I

Warp loom. Wind a shuttle with A and another with B. Following tapestry techniques and sketch (page 100) weave until piece measures 15 (17, 19, 20½, 22½)" (**c** in Measurements), end with both shuttles at left edge.
SHAPE ARMHOLES Weave across 10" (**f**); with another shuttle, weave across remaining threads (**g**) for armhole hem allowance. Work both sections simultaneously for 1", then weave shaded section (**g**) with waste yarn for 2 (2, 2, 3, 3)" (**d**). Weave another 1" hem with A, then continue to weave across all threads for 14 (16, 18, 19, 21)" (**e**) to second armhole and repeat shaping.
Weave 15 (17, 19, 20½, 22½)" (**c**). Remove from loom. Zigzag as shown; do **not** cut and remove waste yarn until after piece is washed and dried.

WEAVING THE FABRIC: WARP II

Wind a shuttle with A and another with B. Weave a piece the same length as the vest, working the Hatching design for about 2" and repeating at even intervals as shown.

FINISHING THE FABRIC: WARPS I AND II

Hand wash in cool water, agitating gently. Rinse and hang to dry. Remove waste yarn. Steam press.

PUTTING IT ALL TOGETHER

Finish armholes and shoulders as on page 97. Pin and attach bottom border using Baseball Stitch (page 15). Try on. Adjust length of front panels as desired, then turn hems to RS and sew by hand. Steam seams flat.

DESIGN CONCEPT

In this version of the Field of Pansies cascading vest, I started with a solid-color warp to create a blank canvas. Using tapestry techniques (page 26), I "painted" free-form bands of colors inspired by weathered, color-streaked rock formations seen in the American Southwest. Because the weaving is worked sideways, the stripes read vertically on the body.

To achieve a longer vest, I wove a separate panel as a border and sewed it to the bottom edge.

THE WOVEN FABRIC: WARP II

Requirements for **12-** OR 12.5-dent heddle

	FOR ALL SIZES				
Width in heddle	3"				
Total warp threads	**36**/38				
Loom waste	24"				
	XS	S	M	L	1X
Warp length	76"	82"	88"	94"	100"

Warp order

A		Hole
	A	Slot

repeat

CLAUDIA HAND PAINT YARNS ADDICTION IN COLORS

A AUBERGINE

B RUBIES PLAYING   **C** SCARLETT O'HARA

D PAGEWOOD FARM SILK RIBBON IN COLOR MISSISSIPPI MUD

WEAVING THE TAPESTRY VEST

The sketches give you some general ideas of shapes and my color use, but feel free to create your own "painting".

- I used 1 row of D, a silk ribbon, to outline each shape.

- Blend colors by Hatching.

- Create curved lines using tapestry techniques as shown below.

- Allow for 1" hems at beginning and end for front edges.

- Match the designs for 3" at the shoulder seams, as shown by the red lines on the sketches.

Curved lines

a Start by building up the bottom shape, decreasing the number of warp threads used by at least 1 each time.

b When you have achieved the desired shape, weave 1 or more rows of a contrasting color, using the tapestry beater or fork to beat the yarn around the shape.

c Now start filling in the top shape. Remember to change the shed for each row and to increase the number of warp threads worked by at least 1 each time. As soon as it is possible, resume using the heddle to beat down the rows.

Hatching

Weave A from right to left and bring the shuttle out somewhere in the middle of the warp. Beat, change the shed, and return the shuttle to the right edge. Change the shed again and weave B from left to right, overlapping A by 2 or more warp threads. Change the shed and return shuttle to left edge. Continue alternating colors, overlapping by as many warp threads as desired. If you find a small "hill" developing, fill in the depression by weaving an extra 2 rows in the matching color.

Tapestry sketches

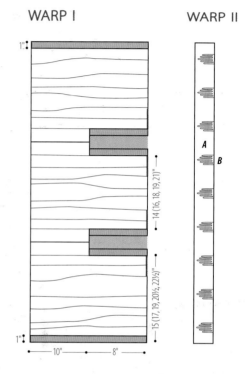

WARP I   WARP II

14 (16, 18, 19, 21)"

15 (17, 19, 20½, 22½)"

10"   8"

A
B

Diagram shows finished fabric measurements.

Matched designs at shoulder

Curved lines

a 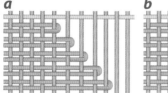   *b* 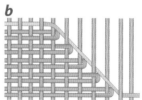   *c*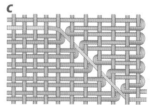

Hatching

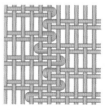

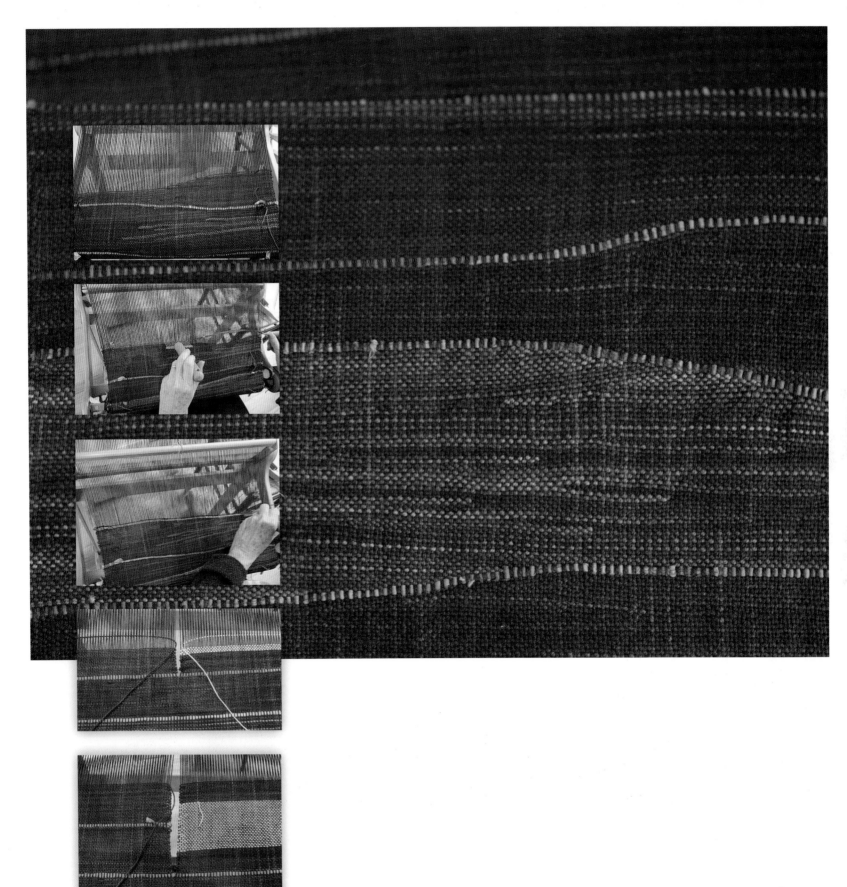

Man vest

WEAVING

KNITTING

SEWING

S (M, L, 1X)
Shown in MEDIUM,
page 103

A 41 (44, 50, 53)"
Measure around chest at
widest point and add 4–6"
for ease.
Woven fronts finish 1"
wider than ½ of back.
B Maximum length 27";
shorten as desired.

10-dent heddle
20" minimum width

2 shuttles

10 warp threads
and 10 weft threads over
plain weave, on the loom

Light weight

A 830 (910, 990,
1060) yds
5 (5, 6, 6) skeins

B 170 (180, 190, 200) yds
1 (1, 1, 2) skeins

C 100 (100, 110, 110) yds
1 skein

Sewing machine with
zigzag capability

THE WOVEN FABRIC

Requirements for 10-dent heddle

	S	M	L	1X
Width in heddle	15¾"	16½"	17½"	18¼"
Total warp threads	158	166	174	182
FOR ALL SIZES				
Loom waste	24"			
Warp length	86"			

Warp order

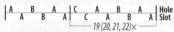

19 (20, 21, 22)×

To prevent tangling when warping 3 colors using the Direct Warping method on a rigid-heddle loom, work as follows: Tie A and B onto back apron bar. **[Pull loop A through first slot, loop B through next slot, loop A through next slot, skip a slot]** across. Cut A and B and tie onto back apron bar. Tie on color C and pull a loop through each skipped slot. Tie off.

Weft order

Start A at right edge (side seam edge) and weave 6 weft picks. Start B at right edge and weave 2 picks. **[Carry up A and weave 6 picks; carry up B and weave 2 picks]** to desired length. Always start and end at right edge to ensure a clean selvedge at the front edge.

WEAVING THE FABRIC

Warp loom. Wind a shuttle with A and another with B. Following the Weft Order, weave until piece measures at least 17". Cut yarn and weave in tails.

SHAPE ARMHOLE Wind a butterfly (page 26) with A and, beginning at right edge, weave across first 34 (38, 44, 50) threads for armhole hem facing (**c**). Continuing in Weft Order, work both sections at the same time for 1" (hem facing), then change butterfly to waste yarn and weave both sections for 13". Weave waste yarn across entire width until warp threads are once again evenly spaced. Weave second piece; it is not necessary to weave in waste for the armhole on the second piece.

Remove from loom; zigzag and cut as shown.

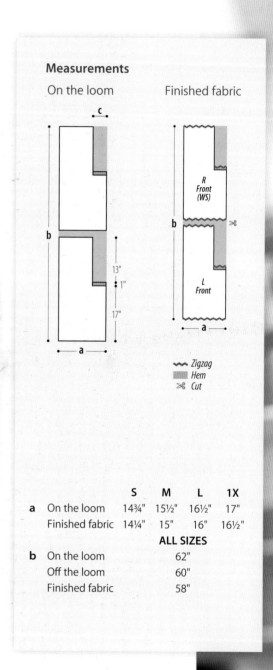

Measurements

On the loom   Finished fabric

		S	M	L	1X
a	On the loom	14¾"	15½"	16½"	17"
	Finished fabric	14¼"	15"	16"	16½"
	ALL SIZES				
b	On the loom	62"			
	Off the loom	60"			
	Finished fabric	58"			

FINISHING THE FABRIC

Hand wash and lay flat to dry.

DESIGN CONCEPT

*This is a shawl-collared vest with a knit back. The front
armholes are shaped on the loom. In order to make the back
wide enough with my 20" loom, I would have had to weave
2 panels, and I worried that the horizontal lines of the plaid
pattern wouldn't align. Knitting the back resolved that issue,
and I think it also makes the design more masculine.*

ROWAN Felted Tweed DK IN COLORS

A 159 Carbon

B 154 Ginger

C 157 Camel

GARTER RIB
MULTIPLE OF 8 + 4
Row 1 (WS) Purl.
Row 2 K4, **[p4, k4]** to end.
Repeat Rows 1 and 2.

PUK
[Pick up and knit a stitch, skip 2 weft threads] to end (page 10).

3.5mm/US4,
3.75mm/US5,
60cm (24") long

10cm/4"

36
22

over Garter Rib, using
smaller needle

&

Sewing needle and
thread

Tapestry needle

Stitch holder

1 closure

See Knitting Basics on
page 10 for unfamiliar
techniques.

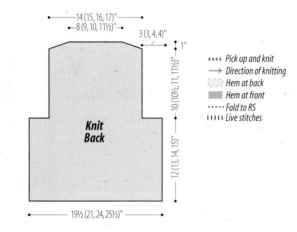

14 (15, 16, 17)"
8 (9, 10, 11½)"
3 (3, 4, 4)"
1"
10 (10½, 11, 11½)"
12 (13, 14, 15)"

**Knit
Back**

19½ (21, 24, 25½)"

•••• Pick up and knit
⟶ Direction of knitting
⫴⫴ Hem at back
▦ Hem at front
- - - Fold to RS
ⅠⅠⅠⅠⅠ Live stitches

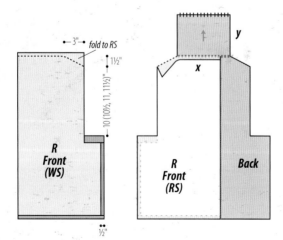

3" fold to RS
1½"
10 (10½, 11, 11½)"

**R
Front
(WS)**

½"

y
x

**R
Front
(RS)**

Back

KNITTING THE BACK
With smaller needle and A, cast on 108 (116, 132, 140). Work in Garter Rib until piece measures 12 (13, 14, 15)" or desired length to armhole, end with Row 2.

SHAPE ARMHOLE At beginning of next 2 rows, bind off 16 (17, 22, 23) — 76 (82, 88, 94) stitches. Continue in pattern until armhole measures 10 (10½, 11, 11½)", end with Row 2. Bind off 4 at beginning of next 8 rows; bind off remaining 44 (50, 56, 62) stitches.

PUTTING IT ALL TOGETHER
Fold woven fabric to WS at side seam edges so underarm width is 3 (3, 4, 4)"; hand sew in place. Trim away top corner (page 15).

Fold armhole hems to WS, then sew by hand.

Fold top edges of front pieces to RS on a diagonal as shown, adjusting the length of the armhole as indicated on schematic for your size, and matching the angle of the knit shoulders. Sew, aligning the plaid.

Sew front and back shoulders together from the RS (see Grafting Weaving to Knitting, page 15).
With A, sew side seams using Mattress Stitch (page 15).
Turn bottom front edges to WS so they match back length, then hem.

KNITTING THE COLLAR
Pick up and knit (PUK) in each bound-off stitch across back neck — 44 (50, 56, 62) stitches. Knit every row until collar measures same length as edge **x** of the woven fronts, end with a RS row. Place stitches on hold. Sew side edges of knit collar (**y**) to edges of right and left fronts (**x**). With larger needle and WS facing, PUK along left front edge, knit held back neck stitches, PUK along right front edge. Knit 1 row. Bind off, taking care to bind off back neck stitches loosely.

KNITTING THE ARMHOLE EDGING
With RS facing, larger needle, A, and beginning at side seam, PUK along woven armhole edge to shoulder seam. Count stitches and PUK same number of stitches along knit armhole edge. Place marker, join, and purl 1 round. Bind off.
Lay vest fronts down, place wet towel on back, and hold steam iron over towel. Allow to dry. Turn over and steam fronts.

FINISHING THE VEST
Try on vest; fold back lapel/band to desired fit. Attach closure through both layers.

Chiffon boa

WEAVING

One size
6" wide (with loops) ×
69" long

10-dent heddle
5" minimum width

1 shuttle

1"

5

10

10 warp threads and 5 weft
threads in plain weave, on
the loom

4

Medium weight
A 80 yds
1 skein

&

1¼ yds chiffon fabric

THE WOVEN FABRIC

Requirements for 10-dent heddle

Width in heddle	2"
Total warp threads	20
Loom waste	20"
Warp length	96"

Warp order

A		Hole
	A	Slot

10×

Weft order
Alternate 1 weft pick A with 1 pick fabric.

WEAVING THE FABRIC

Tear fabric across its width into 2" wide strips. If using 45" wide fabric, each strip of fabric will complete about 9 rows of weaving.

Warp loom. Wind a shuttle with A. Insert a fabric strip into the shed, leaving a 2" tail hanging at the edge. Beat softly, change shed, then weave a row of yarn (see Alternating Colors, page 6). **[Change shed and weave next row with fabric, leaving a 2" loop of fabric at the edge. Change shed and weave next row with yarn]** to end of fabric strip, leaving a 2" tail hanging at the edge. Start a new fabric strip, leaving a 2" tail hanging at opposite edge. Weave until piece measures 76", or desired length. Remove from loom.

FINISHING THE BOA

Across each end of weaving, tie groups of 4 warp threads together in overhand knots (page 9). Trim fringe to even lengths.

Measurements

On the loom   Finished fabric

b   b

a   a

a	On the loom	2", plus loops
b	On the loom	76"
	Off the loom	69"

DESIGN CONCEPT

An easy, fast, fun project. I used hand-dyed tape yarn and tore up strips of a coordinating silky, chiffon fabric. The yarn and fabric alternate in the weft for a very funky scarf.

A PRISM YARNS BON BON IN COLOR ALPINE

FABRIC

Loopy scarf

One size
4" wide × 60" long

12- OR 12.5-dent heddle
5" minimum width

3 shuttles

1"

12 ▦

12 OR **12.5**

12 OR **12.5** warp threads
and 12 weft threads in plain
weave, on the loom

2   **5**

Fine weight

A 175 yds
1 skein

B 60 yds
1 skein

Bulky weight

C 30 yds
1 skein

THE WOVEN FABRIC

Requirements for **12-** OR 12.5-dent heddle

Width in heddle	4½"
Total warp threads	**54**/58
Loom waste	18"
Warp length	80"

Warp order

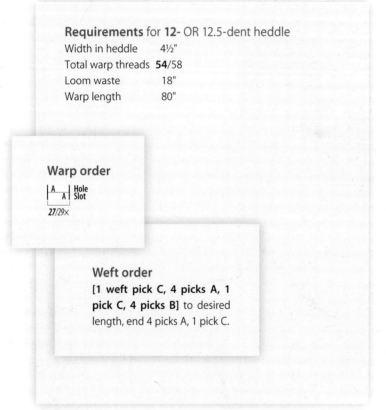

A		Hole
	A	Slot

27/29×

Weft order

[1 weft pick C, 4 picks A, 1 pick C, 4 picks B] to desired length, end 4 picks A, 1 pick C.

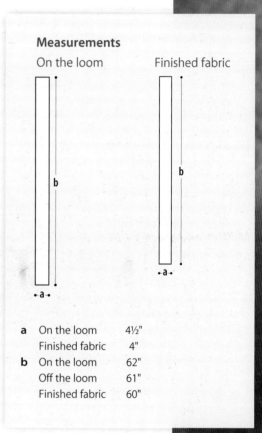

Measurements

On the loom	Finished fabric

a	On the loom	4½"
	Finished fabric	4"
b	On the loom	62"
	Off the loom	61"
	Finished fabric	60"

WEAVING THE FABRIC

Warp loom. Wind a shuttle each with A, B, and C. Beginning with B at left edge, weave 10 picks. Beginning with C at left edge, weave 1 pick C. Beginning with A at right edge, weave 4 picks A. **[Leaving a small loop of C at edge, weave 1 pick C. Carry up B and weave 4 picks B. Leaving a small loop of C at edge, weave 1 pick C. Carry up A and weave 4 picks A]** to end of warp, end 1 pick C, 10 picks B. Remove from loom.

FINISHING THE SCARF

FRINGE Across each end of weaving, tie groups of 4 warp threads together with overhand knots, then twist fringe for 1½" (page 9). Trim fringe to 4".

DESIGN CONCEPT

A simply fun scarf! Loops of the ribbon yarn at the edges make it special.

CLAUDIA HAND PAINTED YARNS Addiction in colors

A Rubies Playing

B Aubergine

C PAGEWOOD FARM Silk Ribbon in color Mississippi Mud

Möbius cowl

THE WOVEN FABRIC

One size

7½" wide × 36" around

10-dent heddle
10" minimum width

3 shuttles

1"

10
10

10 warp threads and 10
weft threads in plain
weave, on the loom

Medium weight

A 80 yds
1 skein

B 100 yds
2 skeins

Super Fine weight

C 90 yds
1 oz

Sewing machine with
zigzag capability

Sewing needle and thread

Tapestry needle

Requirements for 10-dent heddle

Width in heddle	8½"
Total warp threads	84
Loom waste	24"
Warp length	66"

Warp order

B		C		A		B		Hole
	C		A		B		C	Slot

6×   6×   6×   6×
2×

TO WARP THIS LOG CABIN DRAFT ON A RIGID-HEDDLE LOOM using the Direct Warping method (page 6), work as follows:

1 [**(Pull loop C through slot, loop B through hole, skip a slot and hole) 3 times—6 loops/12 warp threads; repeat with B in slot, A in hole; then with A in slot, C in hole]** twice, then [**pull loop C through slot, loop B through hole, skip a slot and hole**] 3 times.

2 After winding onto the back beam and cutting loops, [**remove 1 thread of C from slot and pull it through empty slot next to it**] 3 times. [**Remove 1 thread of B from hole and pull it through empty hole next to it**] 3 times. Repeat for other sections.

Tie onto front. Open shed and insert a pick-up stick or strip of cardboard into the shed BEHIND the heddle and push it all the way to the back beam. This will help maintain a clean shed if warp threads are twisted.

Weft order

[(1 weft pick C, 1 pick B) 10 times, (1 pick B, 1 pick A) 10 times, (1 pick A, 1 pick C) 10 times] to end.

Direct Warping this Log Cabin draft

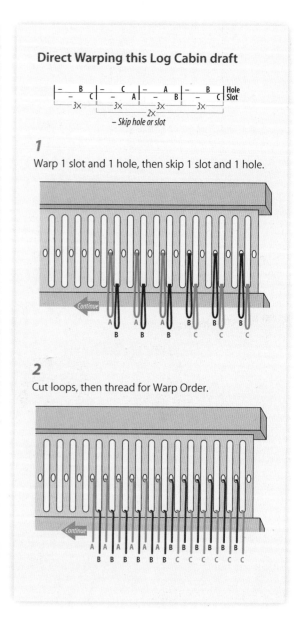

1
Warp 1 slot and 1 hole, then skip 1 slot and 1 hole.

2
Cut loops, then thread for Warp Order.

WEAVING THE FABRIC

Warp loom. Wind a shuttle each with A, B, and C. Following Weft Order, weave until piece measures at least 42". Remove from loom; zigzag raw edges.

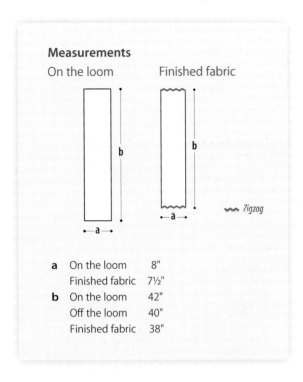

Measurements

	On the loom	Finished fabric

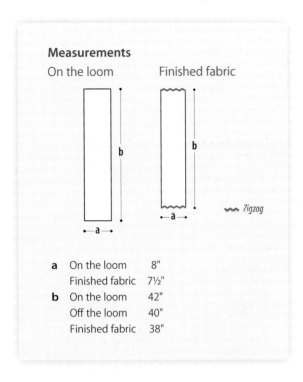

Zigzag

a	On the loom	8"
	Finished fabric	7½"
b	On the loom	42"
	Off the loom	40"
	Finished fabric	38"

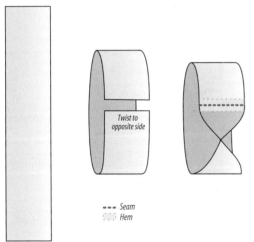

Twist to opposite side

- - - *Seam*
ꝏꝏ *Hem*

FINISHING THE FABRIC

Hand wash in warm water. Wrap in towel to remove excess water and hang to dry.

FINISHING THE COWL

Twist piece once and sew ends together, leaving a 1" seam allowance. Turn under raw edges, then hem (page 15).

DESIGN CONCEPT

Log Cabin describes a technique whereby colors are alternated in the warp and weft in blocks. It's really quite simple, but makes for a very complicated-looking weave structure. No one will believe it's just plain weave on a rigid-heddle loom!

A NORTH LIGHT FIBERS Worsted in color Snow Flake

B TRENDSETTER YARNS Zoe in color 85 Grey Ash

C SILK CITY FIBERS Bambu 7 in color 360 Onyx

Rag bag

WEAVING

SEWING

One size

18" wide × 13" high ×
5" deep

10-dent heddle
20" minimum width

2 shuttles

Tapestry beater
OR kitchen fork

1"

4, 7

10

10 warp threads and 4 weft
threads alternating fabric
and B in plain weave; 7 weft
threads alternating B and C

4 **5**

Medium weight

A 140 yds
1 skein

B 340 yds
4 balls

Bulky weight

C 40 yds
1 skein

&

Sewing machine with
zigzag capability

Sewing needle
and thread

Fabric, 45" wide
D ⅓ yd
E ⅔ yd

Plastic needlepoint canvas
cut to 5½" × 12¾"

2 Bag handles

THE WOVEN FABRIC

Requirements for 10-dent heddle

Width in heddle	20"
Total warp threads	198
Loom waste	24"
Warp length	65"

Warp order

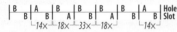

*TO WARP THIS LOG CABIN DRAFT ON A RIGID-HEDDLE
LOOM* using the Direct Warping method shown on page
110, work as follows:

1 **[Pull loop B through slot, loop A through hole, skip a
slot and hole]** 7 times. Pull loop B though next slot. **[Pull
loop A though next slot, loop B through next hole, skip a
slot and hole]** 9 times.
CENTER BLACK STRIPE Pull loop B though every
slot 33 times. **[Pull loop A though next slot,
loop B through next hole, skip a slot and hole]**
9 times. **[Pull loop B through next slot, loop
A through next hole, skip a slot and hole]** 7
times. Pull loop B through next slot.
2 After winding onto the back beam and cutting
loops, remove 1 thread of the color in a slot and
pull it through the empty slot next to it; remove 1
thread of the color in a hole and pull it through a
empty hole next to it; for the center black stripe,
remove 1 thread from slot and pull it through the
empty hole next to it. Ensure that all slots and
holes are filled with the correct color, shifting
threads as necessary. Note that there is an extra
black warp thread at the left edge; allow it to
hang off the back of the loom.

If threads are crossed behind the heddle, open
a shed and insert a pick-up stick or piece of
cardboard into the space BEHIND the heddle. This
will aid in maintaining a clean shed.

Weft order
Work Bands 1–19
(see Alternating Colors,
page 6).

Band	Weft order
19	B, [A, B] 8×
18	B, [C, B] 5×
17	B, [D, B] 4×
16	B, [C, B] 5×
15	B, [E, B] 4×
14	B, [C, B] 5×
13	B, [D, B] 4×
12	B, [C, B] 5×
11	B, [E, B] 4×
10	B, [C, B] 10×
9	B, [E, B] 4×
8	B, [C, B] 5×
7	B, [D, B] 4×
6	B, [C, B] 5×
5	B, [E, B] 4×
4	B, [C, B] 5×
3	B, [D, B] 4×
2	B, [C, B] 5×
1	B, [A, B] 8×

Measurements

On the loom   Finished fabric

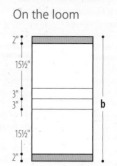
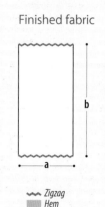

~~~ Zigzag
▓▓ Hem

a On the loom   18"
   Finished fabric   18"
b On the loom   41"
   Off the loom   31½"
   Finished fabric   31½"

WEAVING THE FABRIC

Warp loom. Wind a shuttle with B and
another with C. Weave, following the
Weft Order.

To weave with fabric strips

Cut or tear each fabric across its width
into eight 1½" strips. Each strip of fabric
will complete 2 rows of weaving. Fold
strip in half lengthwise with RS out and
insert into shed, leaving a tail; weave
tail back into same shed. Beat hard;
to get a tighter weave, use a tapestry
beater or fork. Change shed and weave
second half of strip. Weave tail of fabric
back into same shed. Start next strip
at opposite edge from previous strip.
Remove from loom; zigzag raw edges.

DESIGN CONCEPT

Alternating dark and light warp threads and weaving with fabric strips and a heavy yarn creates an interesting, sturdy tote bag with lots of texture. I used 2 fabrics — one a mottled black/brown batik and the other a print with grays and black. The resulting woven fabric looks complex and richly textured.

PUTTING IT ALL TOGETHER

With WS together, fold piece end to end. With B, sew side edges together using Mattress Stitch (page 15) between first and second warp threads. Turn hems to WS; fold under raw edge and with B, sew. Fold up bottom corners as indicated and sew in place.

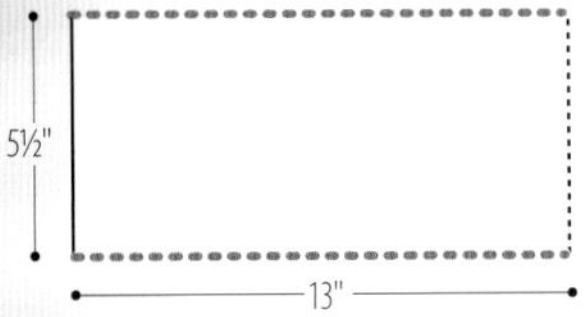

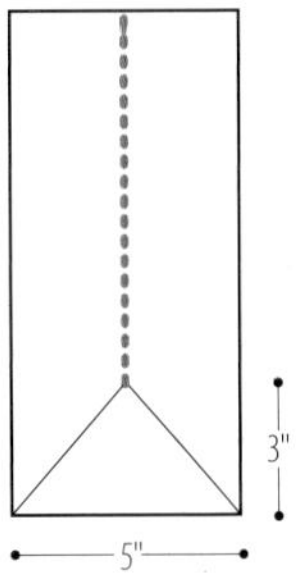

FINISHING THE BAG

With B, sew handles, sewing through both layers at hems. Cut a piece of fabric 6½" X 28" and sew a cover for the plastic canvas. Place in bottom of bag.

A KOLLAGE Riveting Worsted in color 8105 Sand Denim

B ROWAN Handknit Cotton in color 252 Black

C TRENDSETTER YARNS Kinetic in color 07 Latte

D Fabric

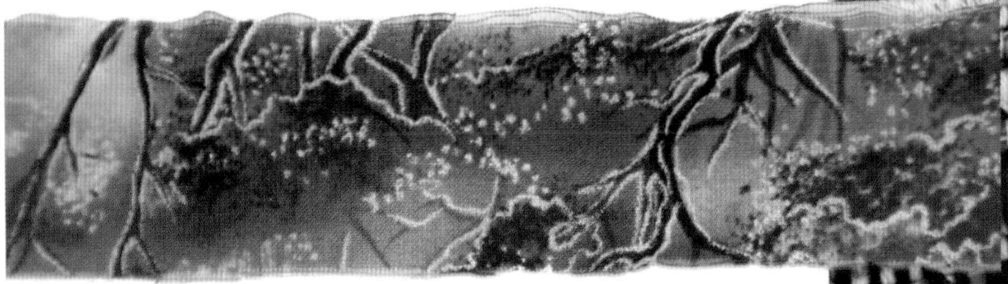

E Fabric

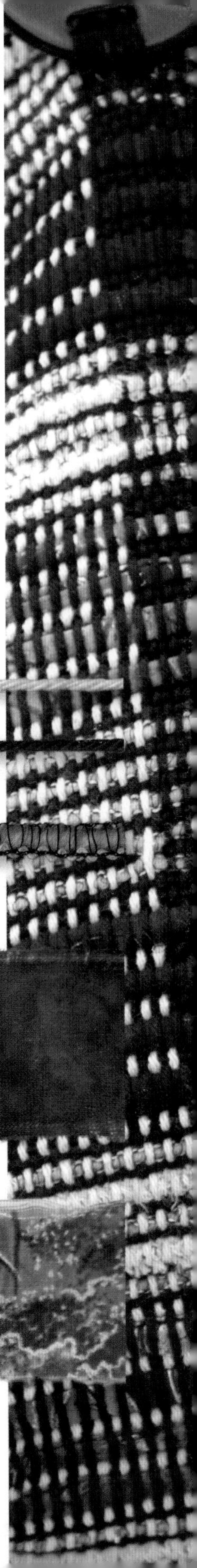

S (M, L)
Shown in MEDIUM

20 (22, 24)" in
circumference
12" high

12- OR 12.5-dent heddle
15" minimum width

2 shuttles

1"

12
12 OR 12.5

12 OR 12.5 warp threads
and 12 weft threads in plain
weave, on the loom

Light weight
A 140 yds
1 skein

B and **C** 80 yds each
1 skein each

Super Fine weight
D 220 yds
2 oz

4mm/US6,
40cm (16") long

10cm/4"

28
21
over stockinette

 &

Sewing machine with
zigzag capability

Sewing needle and thread

Stitch marker

Tapestry needle

See Knitting Basics on
page 10 for unfamiliar
techniques.

Three hats

THE WOVEN FABRIC

Requirements for **12-** OR **12.5-dent heddle**

Width in heddle	15"
Total warp threads	**180**/188
Loom waste	24"
Warp length	54"

Warp order

D		A	Hole
	D		A	Slot

—45/47×—

Weft order
Alternate 1 weft pick B with 1 pick D.

Measurements

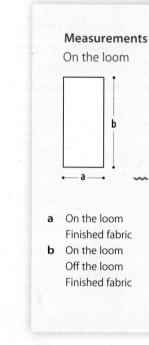 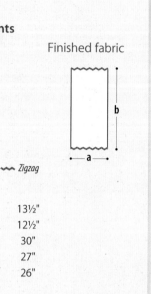

On the loom   Finished fabric

~~~ Zigzag

a	On the loom	13½"	
	Finished fabric	12½"	
b	On the loom	30"	
	Off the loom	27"	
	Finished fabric	26"	

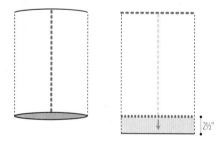

→ Direction of knitting
•••• Pick up and knit
--- Seam
▓▓ Knitting

2½"

PUK
[Pick up and knit a stitch,
skip 2 weft threads] to end
(page 10). Count stitches and
increase or decrease to required
number on the next row.

WEAVING THE FABRIC
Warp loom. Wind a shuttle with B and another with D. Following the
Weft Order, weave until piece measures at least 30". Remove from
loom; zigzag raw edges.

FINISHING THE FABRIC
Hand wash in warm water. Wrap in towel to remove excess water and
hang to dry.

PUTTING IT ALL TOGETHER
Sew ends together, adjusting length to desired head circumference.
Leaving 1" seam allowances, trim away excess fabric. Turn under raw
edges, then hem (page 15).

KNITTING THE BAND
With RS facing, circular needle, C, and beginning at back seam, PUK
around lower edge (page 10). Place marker and join to work in the
round. Knit 1 round. **[Purl 5 rounds, knit 5 rounds]** twice, purl 5
rounds. Bind off loosely in knit.

FINISHING THE HAT
Cut a 30" length of yarn, thread it through a tapestry needle, and work
a running stitch around the top edge of the hat. Gather tightly and
secure tails.

DESIGN CONCEPT

Make a simple rectangle with a knit band. Try it with any yarn and pattern. For this version, I simply gathered the top. Fold it, twist it, pin it — wear it any way you like!

MANOS DEL URUGUAY SILK BLEND IN COLORS

A 3110 STELLAR

B 3043 JUNIPER   **C** 3008 BLACK

D SILK CITY FIBERS BAMBU 7 IN COLOR 360 ONYX

THE WOVEN FABRIC

Requirements
for 10-dent heddle

Width in heddle	14½"
Total warp threads	144
Loom waste	24"
Warp length	52"

Weft order

Band	Weft order	
6	[A, C]	8×
5	[B, A]	8×
4	[B, C]	4×
3	[A, C]	8×
2	[B, A]	4×
1	[C, B]	8×

Warp order

```
 C   A   B  Hole
   A   B   C  Slot
 └8×┘└8×┘└8×┘
      └3×┘
```

TO WARP THIS LOG CABIN DRAFT ON A RIGID-HEDDLE LOOM using the Direct Warping method shown on page 110, work as follows:

1 [(**Pull loop C through slot, loop B through hole, skip a slot and hole) 4 times — 8 loops/16 warp threads; repeat with B in slot, A in hole; then with A in slot, C in hole]** 3 times.
2 After winding onto the back beam and cutting loops, [**remove 1 thread of C from slot and pull it through empty slot next to it**] 8 times. [**Remove 1 thread of B from hole and pull it through empty hole next to it**] 8 times. Repeat for other sections.

Tie onto front. Open shed and insert a pick-up stick or strip of cardboard into the shed BEHIND the heddle and push it all the way to the back beam. This will help maintain a clean shed if warp threads are twisted.

WEAVING THE FABRIC

Warp loom. Wind a shuttle each with A, B, and C. Following the Weft Order, weave until piece measures at least 30". Remove from loom; zigzag raw edges.

Follow directions on page 114 for Finishing the Fabric, Putting It All Together, and Knitting the Band EXCEPT PUK with A AND knit 1 round, adjusting to a multiple of 4, work in k2, p2 rib for 2½", then bind off loosely in pattern.

FINISHING THE HAT

Sew top edge closed using Baseball Stitch (page15).

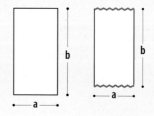

Measurements

	On the loom	Finished fabric
a	On the loom	13½"
	Finished fabric	13"
b	On the loom	28"
	Off the loom	26"
	Finished fabric	25"

〰 Zigzag

A PLYMOUTH YARNS Baby Alpaca Worsted in color 500 Black

B TRENDSETTER YARNS Zoe in color 85 Grey Ash

C SILK CITY FIBERS Bambu 7 in color 360 Onyx

WEAVING

KNITTING

SEWING

S (M, L)
Show in SMALL

20 (21½, 23)" in circumference
12" high

10-dent heddle
15" minimum width

3 shuttles

1"

10 ▦
10

10 warp threads and 10 weft threads in plain weave, on the loom

1 **4**

Medium weight
A 240 yds
3 skeins

B 120 yds
2 skeins

Super Fine weight
C 120 yds
1 oz

4.5mm/US7,
40cm (16") long

10cm/4"

28 ▦
20

over k2, p2 rib

&

Sewing machine with zigzag capability

Sewing needle and thread

Stitch marker

Tapestry needle

See Knitting Basics on page 10 for unfamiliar techniques.

THE WOVEN FABRIC

S (M, L)
Shown in SMALL

19 (20, 21)" in
circumference
10½" high

10-dent heddle
12" minimum width

2 shuttles

1"

8
10

10 warp threads
and 8 weft threads in plain
weave, on the loom

Fine weight

A 50 yds
1 ball

B and **C 120 yds each**
2 balls each

4mm/US6,
40cm (16") long

10cm/4"

24 ▦
17

over k2, p2 rib

&

Sewing machine with
zigzag capability

Sewing needle and thread

Stitch marker

Tapestry needle

See Knitting Basics on
page 10 for unfamiliar
techniques.

Warp order

| B | | C | | B | | Hole |
| | B | | C | | B | Slot |

end ⟶ 27× ⟵

Weft order

Alternate 2 weft picks
B with 2 picks C.

Requirements for 10-dent heddle

Width in heddle	11"
Total warp threads	110
Loom waste	24"
Warp length	50"

Measurements

	On the loom	Finished fabric

a	On the loom	10"
	Finished fabric	9½"
b	On the loom	26"
	Off the loom	25"
	Finished fabric	23"

∿ Zigzag

WEAVING THE FABRIC

Warp loom. Wind a shuttle with B and another with C. Following the Weft Order, weave until piece measures at least 26". Remove from loom; zigzag raw edges.

Follow directions on page 114 for Finishing the Fabric, Putting It All Together, and Knitting the Band EXCEPT PUK with A AND knit 1 round, adjusting to a multiple of 4 AND work in k2, p2 rib for 5 rounds, knit 8 rounds, then bind off loosely in pattern.

FINISHING THE HAT

Cut a 20" length of A, thread it through a tapestry needle, and work a running stitch around the top of the hat, 2" from the edge. Gather tightly and secure tails.

CLASSIC ELITE Jil Eaton CottonTail in colors

A 7532 Plum

B 7588 Bittersweet   **C** 7585 Orangini

The totes

One Size

✳ 12" tall (excluding
handles) × 10 (17)" wide
× 4 (3)" deep

7.5- OR 8-dent heddle
12 (20)" minimum width

2 (4) shuttles

1"

8
7.5 OR 8

7.5 OR 8 warp threads and
8 weft threads in plain
weave, on the loom

Medium weight

Small tote
A and B 120 yds each
1 skein each

Large tote
A, B, C, D 125 yds each
1 skein each

&

Sewing machine with
zigzag capability

✳ If different, instructions
for Small tote are given
first, followed by Large tote
in parentheses.

THE WOVEN FABRIC

Requirements for **7.5**- OR 8-dent heddle

	SMALL TOTE	LARGE TOTE
Width in heddle	**11¾"**/11"	**19¾"**/18½"
Total warp threads	88	148
Loom waste	24"	24"
Warp length	54"	54"

Warp order: Large tote

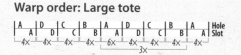

Warp order: Small tote

B	A	Hole
B	A	Slot
22×	22×	

Weft order: Large tote

12 weft picks A, **[8
picks each B, C,
D, and A]** 6 times,
8 picks each B, C,
and D, 12 picks A.

Weft order: Small tote

24 weft picks A, 32 picks B, 6 picks
A, 6 picks B, 13" A, 6 picks B, 6 picks
A, 32 picks B, 24 picks A.

Measurements

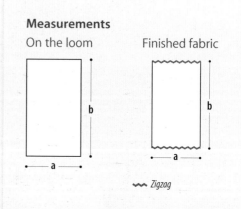

On the loom   Finished fabric

〰 *Zigzag*

		SMALL TOTE	LARGE TOTE
a	On the loom	**11"**/10"	**18½"**/17¼"
	Finished fabric	**10"**/9¼"	**17"**/15¾"
b	On the loom	30"	30"
	Off the loom	29"	29"
	Finished fabric	28"	28"

WEAVING THE FABRIC
SMALL AND LARGE TOTES

Warp loom. Wind a shuttle in each color. Weave, following
the Weft Order. Remove from loom; zigzag raw edges.

FINISHING THE FABRIC
SMALL AND LARGE TOTES

Wash in machine on gentle cycle (warm wash, cold rinse)
with a few drops of dishwashing liquid. Lay flat to dry.

DESIGN CONCEPT

If you have a smaller loom, knitting can be used to expand the size of your piece. For these totes, I wove the center panels and knit the side gussets. A knit flower embellishes the large tote.

LARGE TOTE

MANOS DEL URUGUAY WOOL CLÀSICA IN COLORS

A 54 BRICK   **B** 68 CITRIC

C G COFFEE   **D** 51 JADE

SMALL TOTE

MANOS DEL URUGUAY WOOL CLÀSICA IN COLORS

A U RUST   **B** 49 HENNA

5mm/US8,
60cm (24") long

10cm/4"

32 (24)

17 (18)

over Garter (Woven) Stitch

&

Sewing needle
and thread

Tapestry needle

1 yd lining fabric

1 yd medium weight fusible
interfacing

1 pair bag handles

OPTIONAL
Plastic needlepoint canvas

See Knitting Basics on
page 10 for unfamiliar
techniques.

PUK

[Pick up and knit a stitch, skip 2
weft threads] to end (page 10).

WOVEN STITCH

OVER AN ODD NUMBER OF STITCHES
Row 1 (RS) K1, **[slip 1 with yarn in front
(wyif), k1]** to end. *Row 2 and all WS
rows* Purl. *Rows 3, 7* Knit. *Row 5* K2, **[sl 1
wyif, k1]** to last stitch, k1. *Row 8* Purl.
Repeat Rows 1–8.

KNITTING THE GUSSETS: SMALL (LARGE) TOTE

Turn zigzagged edges to WS, then hem. Mark 12 (12½)" down from
top edge on each side. With RS facing and A (D), pick up and knit (PUK)
between top edge and marker.

FOR SMALL TOTE Work in garter stitch in following color pattern: 1 row
A, 2 rows B, 2 rows A, 2 rows B, 16 rows A, **[2 rows B, 2 rows A]** twice.

FOR LARGE TOTE With D, knit 2 rows, adjusting to an odd number of
stitches if necessary. Purl 1 row. With B, work Rows 1–4 of Woven Stitch.
With C, work Rows 5–8. Knit 1 row, purl 1 row. With B, work Rows 1–4.
With D, work Rows 5–7. Purl 1 row.

FOR BOTH TOTES Bind off.
Repeat for other side.

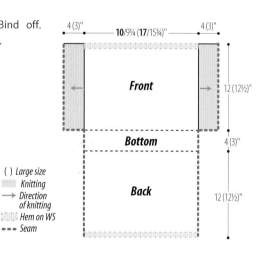

4 (3)" **10/9¼ (17/15¾)"** 4 (3)"

Front 12 (12½)"

Bottom 4 (3)"

Back 12 (12½)"

( ) *Large size*
Knitting
→ *Direction
of knitting*
Hem on WS
--- *Seam*

KNITTING THE FLOWER

With B, cast on 4, leaving a long tail. Knit 1 row. *Row 1* Cast on 4. K8.
Rows 2–4 Knit. *Row 5* Bind off 4, knit to end. *Row 6* K4. Work Rows
1–6 five more times, then work Rows 1–4 once more. Bind off all
stitches. Cut yarn, leaving a long tail. With tapestry needle, thread
tail through straight side edge, gather into a flower shape, and fasten off. Sew half of cast-on edge to half of bound-off edge. Cut yarn,
leaving a long tail.

FLOWER CENTER With A, cast on 2. **[Kf&b]** twice — 4 stitches. *Row 1*
Knit. *Row 2* **[K2tog]** twice — 2 stitches. Slip first stitch over second
stitch to bind off. Cut yarn, leaving a long tail, and fasten off. With
tapestry needle, thread both tails through center of flower. Leave all
tails for attaching flower to bag.

Sew flower to bag in desired location, sewing only through woven
fabric and not lining. Weave tails through back of petals, securing
them to fabric but leaving petal edges unsewn.

PUTTING IT ALL TOGETHER

Pin fusible interfacing to WS of bag. Trace around bag shape, leaving bound-off stitches of knitting exposed. If interfacing isn't wide enough, cut separate pieces for the gussets. Cut out shape and fuse interfacing to WS of woven and knitted fabric. Graft bound-off edges of gussets together (page 15). Sew bottom edges of gusset to bottom edges of bag using Baseball Stitch (page 15).

Attach lining and handles and add optional bottom support as shown in Steps 7 and 8.

LINING YOUR BAG

1 Measure bag for lining dimensions.

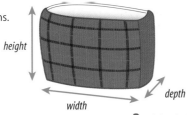

height

depth

width

2 Cut lining fabric 1" larger than measurements.

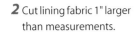

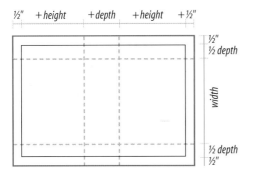

| ½" | + height | + depth | + height | + ½" |

½"
½ depth

width

½ depth
½"

3 Fold in half and sew sides.

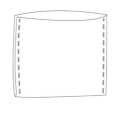

4 Make paper bag corners:

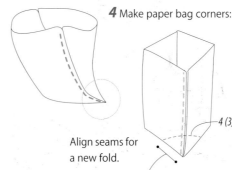

Align seams for a new fold.

Measure 2 (1½)" from seam and sew across point. Repeat at other seam.

4 (3)"

5 Tack points under.

6 Fold top edge to WS.

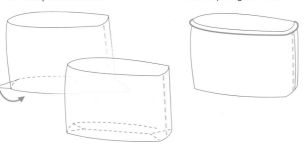

7 Insert lining into bag and stitch to inside edge of bag. (Remember to fold woven edges to inside of bag.)

8 Center bottom of handle approximately 2" from top edge of bag. Using yarn, sew through all layers. Repeat with other handle on other side.

Optional: Measure bottom and add a piece of plastic canvas to support bottom of bag.

Clutch

12- OR 12.5-dent heddle
12" minimum width

2 shuttles

1"

12

12 OR 12.5

12 OR 12.5 warp threads
and 12 weft threads in plain
weave, on the loom

Medium weight

A 95 yds, 1 skein

B 50 yds, 1 skein

Super Fine weight

C 120 yds, 1 oz

Sewing machine with
zigzag capability

Sewing needle and thread

Lining fabric 12" X 18"

Woven fusible interfacing
in black 11" X 16"

Piece of batting 11" X 16"

Plastic needlepoint canvas,
cut to 8" X 10"

White pencil or chalk

Straight pins

Large snap

Button thread

Tapestry needle

OPTIONAL
3.5mm/US4 knitting
needles
Decorative pin or button

THE WOVEN FABRIC

**Requirements for 12
OR 12.5-dent heddle**

Width in heddle **12½"**/12"
Total warp threads 150
Loom waste 24"
Warp length 42"

Weft order

Alternate 1 weft pick A
with 1 pick C.

Measurements

On the loom Finished fabric

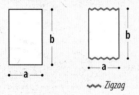

Zigzag

a On the loom 11"
   Finished fabric 10"
b On the loom 18"
   Off the loom 17"
   Finished fabric 16"

Warp order

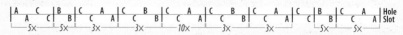

WEAVING THE FABRIC

Warp loom. Wind a shuttle with A and another with C. Following the Weft Order, weave until piece measures at least 18". Remove from loom; zigzag raw edges.

FINISHING THE FABRIC

Wash in cold water with a few drops of dishwashing liquid. Rinse in cold water and lay flat to dry.

PUTTING IT ALL TOGETHER

1 Draw pattern dimensions onto interfacing.

2 Align and fuse interfacing to WS of woven fabric.

3 Stack onto lining with RS together and interfacing on top, and pin together.

4 Cut to shape.

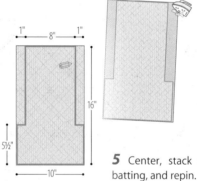

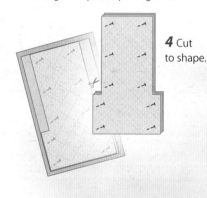

5 Center, stack onto batting, and repin.

6 Cut batting.

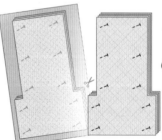

Cut
Seam
Interfacing
Fabric WS
Fabric RS
Lining
Batting
Plastic

7 Sew ¼" seam around edges, leaving base of bag unstitched.

8 Turn RS out.

9 Insert 8" × 10" plastic canvas (trim if needed).

DESIGN CONCEPT

Simple stripes in the warp create a classy clutch. Quilt batting and a piece of plastic needlepoint canvas sandwiched between the weaving and lining give the bag body and shape. The yarn has a satiny feel and interesting texture. Alternating it with a thinner bamboo yarn creates a richly textured textile, perfect for an evening clutch. A shimmery black satin lining and decorative pin complete the party look.

10 Tack plastic canvas in place at **x**, then sew opening closed.

11 Fold and sew gussets using Blind Stitch (page 15).

12 Optional: Add handle. With purl side out, sew one end to inside of bag at **y** and other end to outside at **y**.

13 Pinch gusset at opening and sew in place for 1". Repeat for second side (with or without handle).

14 Add snap to center of flap and front of bag. (Add pin or button to outer flap if desired.)

KNITTING THE HANDLE *OPTIONAL*

With C, cast on 65. Beginning with a purl row, work 5 rows in stockinette. Bind off. Cut yarn, leaving a long tail; fasten off.

BERROCO CAPTIVA IN COLORS

A 5534 NOTTE   **B** 5546 STEEL

C SILK CITY FIBERS BAMBU 7 IN COLOR 360 ONYX

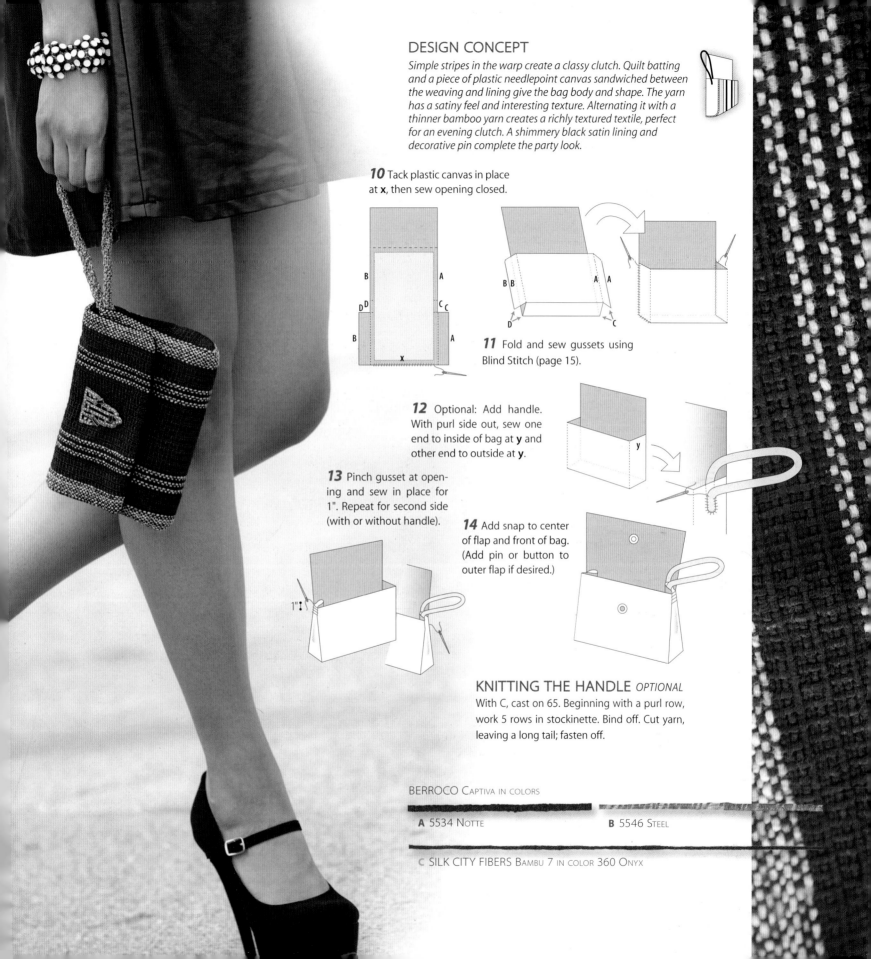

Baby sack

WEAVING

KNITTING

SEWING

One size

28" around (14" wide ×
21" long)

7.5- OR 8-dent heddle
15" minimum width

4 shuttles

1"

8
7.5 OR 8

7.5 OR 8 warp threads
and 8 weft threads in plain
weave, on the loom

Medium weight

A **200 yds**
1 ball

D **75 yds**
1 ball

Light weight

B **420 yds**
4 balls

C **30 yds**
1 ball

&

Sewing machine with
zigzag capability

THE WOVEN FABRIC

Requirements for **7.5-** OR 8-dent heddle

Width in heddle	**13½"**/13¼"
Total warp threads	**102**/106
Loom waste	24"
Warp length	72"

Warp order

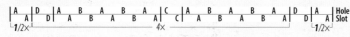

Weft order

**[Weave 14 weft picks randomly using A and B and using
Hatching technique occasionally for a watercolor effect
(page 26)]**, weave 2 picks C. Work from **[** to **]** once more, then
weave 2 picks D.

Measurements

On the loom   Finished fabric

〰 *Zigzag*

a	On the loom	12"
	Finished fabric	11½"
b	On the loom	48"
	Off the loom	46"
	Finished fabric	43"

WEAVING THE FABRIC

Warp loom. Wind a shuttle each with A, B, C, and D. Following the Weft
Order, weave until piece measures at least 48". Remove from loom; zigzag
raw edges.

FINISHING THE FABRIC

Hand wash in cool water and place in dryer on low heat until almost dry.
Remove from dryer and, while still damp, steam press with a cloth.

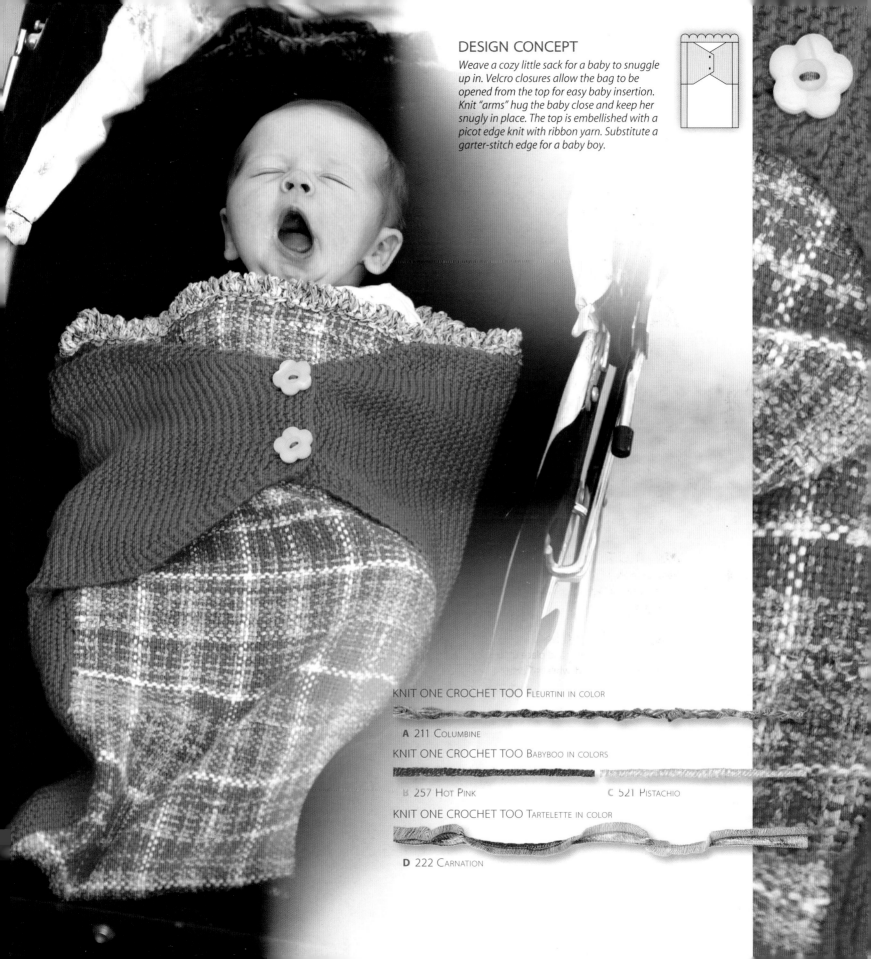

DESIGN CONCEPT

Weave a cozy little sack for a baby to snuggle up in. Velcro closures allow the bag to be opened from the top for easy baby insertion. Knit "arms" hug the baby close and keep her snugly in place. The top is embellished with a picot edge knit with ribbon yarn. Substitute a garter-stitch edge for a baby boy.

KNIT ONE CROCHET TOO Fleurtini in color

A 211 Columbine

KNIT ONE CROCHET TOO Babyboo in colors

B 257 Hot Pink   **C** 521 Pistachio

KNIT ONE CROCHET TOO Tartelette in color

D 222 Carnation

PUK

[Pick up and knit a stitch, skip 2 weft threads or 3 warp threads] to end (page 10). Count stitches and increase or decrease to required number on the next row.

DEC 1

At beginning of row K2, SSK.
At end of row K2tog, k2.

PICOT EDGE

[K2tog, yo] to last 2, k2tog.

PUTTING IT ALL TOGETHER

Turn under top edge, then hem. Hem other end so finished measurement is 40½".

KNITTING THE BORDERS AND ARMS

LEFT BORDER/ARM With RS facing, smaller needle, and B, pick up and knit (PUK) along left edge of weaving. Knit 12 rows. **Next row** (WS) Bind off until 49 stitches remain on left needle, knit to end—50 stitches. Knit 28 rows. Dec 1 each side every RS row 13 times—24 stitches. **Next RS row: Buttonhole row** (RS) K2, SSK, k2, bind off 2, k7, bind off 2, k1, k2tog, k2. **Next row** Work across, casting on 2 above bound-off stitches. Dec 1 each side every RS row 3 times—16 stitches. Bind off in knit.

RIGHT BORDER/ARM PUK along right edge of weaving and knit 12 rows. **Next row** (WS) K50, bind off remaining stitches. Rejoin yarn and work as for left border/arm, eliminating buttonholes.

TOP BORDERS With RS facing, larger needle, and D, PUK across top of border, top edge of weaving, and top of other border. Knit 2 rows, adjusting to an even number of stitches on the first row. Purl 1 row. Work Picot Edge. Purl 1 row, knit 1 row, purl 1 row. Bind off, leaving a 24" tail for seaming. Fold edging to inside along picot edge and sew in place. Repeat for remaining edge.

FINISHING THE SACK

Fold piece up so picot edges meet. From RS, with B, sew side edges from fold to arms using an overhand stitch (page 15). Sew 9" strips of Velcro to open edges along base of arms. Sew 2 buttons to right arm.

3.75mm/US5
5.5mm/US9,
60cm (24") long

10cm/4"

40 | | 20

over garter stitch, using smaller needle and B

10cm/4"

24 | | 16

over stockinette stitch, using larger needle and D

&

Sewing needle and thread
Tapestry needle
20" sew-on Velcro
2 25mm (1") buttons

See Knitting Basics on page 10 for unfamiliar techniques.

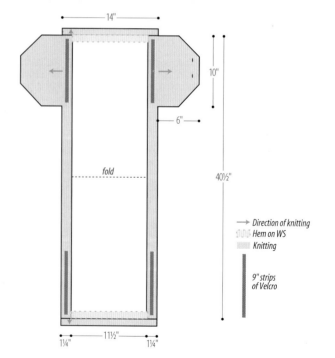

14"

10"

6"

fold

40½"

11½"

1¼"   1¼"

→ Direction of knitting
Hem on WS
Knitting

9" strips of Velcro

weave • knit • wear

127

A gallery of multi-shaft loom projects

Though the directions in this book are tailored to the rigid-heddle weaver, the designs are useful to all weavers. The shapes are simple, require little cutting and sewing, and are perfect vehicles to display the fabulous textiles you can create with a multi-shaft loom. You need not feel confined by the fibers and setts that I have used. Because you have a broader range of setts, you have a greater choice of yarns. Your looms also allow for longer warps. Feel free to combine pieces that I have done on separate warps into one. I encourage you to explore the myriad design possibilities available to you to create unique garments of your own.

I invited 6 weavers from the Weavers' Guild of Boston to create fabrics for 6 of the design concepts in this book. They worked with 5- to 8-shaft weave structures, hand-dyed warps and wefts, and as many as 60 ends per inch to create fabrics to my garment specifications. They are dazzling! I hope they inspire you.

Barbara Herbster

The combination of Barbara's plaited twill pattern and choice of colors has a very cool, Southwestern feel to it, which is enhanced by her choice of colors. For the front panels she used a different treadling and incorporated recyled sari silk yarn and turquoise beads. Because the vest is woven sideways, from front edge to front edge, these details read vertically for a figure-flattering, knock-out vest. Starting with a weaving width of 30", this vest has a finished length of 24".

Field of pansies (page 96)
Weave structure: Plaited Twill (*A Weaver's Book of 8-Shaft Patterns: From the Friends of Handwoven*, edited by Carol Strickler).
Fibers: VALLEY YARNS 8/2 Tencel, JAGGERSPUN Zephyr Wool-Silk, WOOL PEDDLER 2/18 Sari Silk.
Sett: 24 epi.
Finishing: Hand washed in cool water. Spun in washer and placed in dryer for 30 minutes. Ironed while damp and laid flat to dry.

Ruth Buchman

Ruth wove this fabric years ago as the result of a workshop. By warping the space-dyed ribbon on a separate shaft, she created warp floats that sparkle against the lush chenille background. Amazingly, and fortunately for me, she had woven panels of fabric that were just the right width and length for the Shawl-Collared Ruana. The pieces came together perfectly; it was a match made in heaven!

Shawl-collared ruana (page 42)

Weave structure: Plain weave with supplementary warp on 5 shafts.
Fibers: Printed ribbon, rayon chenille from SILK CITY FIBERS in 5 colors, 8/2 unmercerized cotton in 1 color, mill ends.

Sett: 18 epi with cotton alternating with chenille.
Finishing: Hand washed in lukewarm water with a few drops of fabric softener added to the last rinse. Spun out in washing machine. Dried in machine on medium, then laid flat to dry.

weave • knit • wear

Rita Steinbach

The more I look at Rita's fabric and how she designed it, the more intrigued I become. It is double weave, with a hand-painted warp for the top layer; the bottom layer features bands of more subtle colors. When they interconnect they create a contemporary, bold pattern. The fact that there are 2 layers allows for a clever way to join the pieces: Rita sewed them together, interweaving the layers of the panels.

Liquid gold (page 40)
Weave structure: Double weave on 8 shafts.
Fibers: Bottom layer: 8/2 and 10/2 Tencel; top layer: 8/2 cotton/rayon hand-painted warp; weft 2/18 JAGGERSPUN Zephyr Wool-Silk.
Sett: 48 epi (24 epi each layer).
Finishing: Hand washed, then hung to dry.

Deborah Kaplan

Debbie's fabric takes my breath away. She hand dyed very fine silk. The warp is 3 colors, shading from purple to fuchsia. The weft is 4 colors, shading from mustard to leaf green. Threaded in a point-twill pattern of her own design, and sett and woven at 60 ends per inch, the result is iridescent. Because 1 side is more weft faced and the other is more warp faced, the contrast between the 2 sides is striking. In order to show as many of the color variations as possible, I used 1 side for the left front and the other for the right.

Tweedy shirt (page 62)
Weave structure: 4/1/1/2 point twill on 8 shafts. Some threads in both warp and weft are tripled, which skews the diamond shapes and makes them look more complicated than they actually are.
Fibers: 60/2 silk, hand-dyed with Washfast acid dyes.
Sett: 60 epi.
Finishing: Hand washed in warm water. Hung to dry.

131

Dorothy Solbrig

I am impressed by the thoughtfulness behind Dorothy's fabric. She wove all of her panels on 1 warp, using a different tie-up, treadling, and weft color for the center panel than for the side panels. She achieved 2 different yet coordinating fabrics; the center panel has a strong horizontal pattern, while the side panels feature subtle vertical stripes. The delicate neckline detail was created by using a separate bobbin of color for each motif. The Tencel fabric has a lovely sheen, and I made it shorter than my original for a dressier style.

Pontunic (page 50)

Weave structure: 8-shaft twill variations.
Fiber: 8/2 Tencel.
Sett: 25 epi.
Finishing: Hand washed with a few drops of fabric softener added to the last rinse. Dried in dryer until damp. Pressed and laid flat to dry.

Patricia Flaherty

Pat's fabric reads to me like a beautiful, abstract, landscape painting. The subtle shadings of her hand-painted warp interact with the weave structure so the pattern blocks seem to dissolve at times. The rayon fabric has a lustrous look and drape, creating a totally different look than my wool version.

Aegean tunic (page 54)

Weave structure: Modified 4-shaft crackle weave with 1 shuttle, alternating 4 blocks in threading and treadling.
Fiber: 6-ply rayon, hand-dyed with PRO Chemical & Dye MX cold-water dyes.
Sett: 16 epi.
Finishing: Machine washed, gentle cycle, warm water. Dried until damp in dryer. Steam pressed.

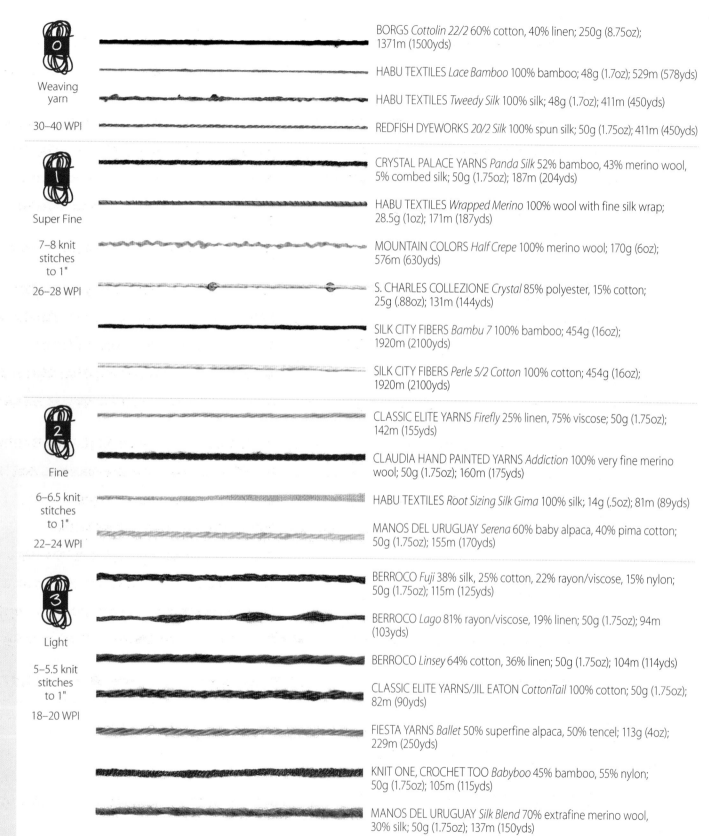

BORGS *Cottolin 22/2* 60% cotton, 40% linen; 250g (8.75oz); 1371m (1500yds)

HABU TEXTILES *Lace Bamboo* 100% bamboo; 48g (1.7oz); 529m (578yds)

HABU TEXTILES *Tweedy Silk* 100% silk; 48g (1.7oz); 411m (450yds)

REDFISH DYEWORKS *20/2 Silk* 100% spun silk; 50g (1.75oz); 411m (450yds)

Weaving yarn

30–40 WPI

CRYSTAL PALACE YARNS *Panda Silk* 52% bamboo, 43% merino wool, 5% combed silk; 50g (1.75oz); 187m (204yds)

HABU TEXTILES *Wrapped Merino* 100% wool with fine silk wrap; 28.5g (1oz); 171m (187yds)

MOUNTAIN COLORS *Half Crepe* 100% merino wool; 170g (6oz); 576m (630yds)

S. CHARLES COLLEZIONE *Crystal* 85% polyester, 15% cotton; 25g (.88oz); 131m (144yds)

SILK CITY FIBERS *Bambu 7* 100% bamboo; 454g (16oz); 1920m (2100yds)

SILK CITY FIBERS *Perle 5/2 Cotton* 100% cotton; 454g (16oz); 1920m (2100yds)

Super Fine

7–8 knit stitches to 1"

26–28 WPI

CLASSIC ELITE YARNS *Firefly* 25% linen, 75% viscose; 50g (1.75oz); 142m (155yds)

CLAUDIA HAND PAINTED YARNS *Addiction* 100% very fine merino wool; 50g (1.75oz); 160m (175yds)

HABU TEXTILES *Root Sizing Silk Gima* 100% silk; 14g (.5oz); 81m (89yds)

MANOS DEL URUGUAY *Serena* 60% baby alpaca, 40% pima cotton; 50g (1.75oz); 155m (170yds)

Fine

6–6.5 knit stitches to 1"

22–24 WPI

BERROCO *Fuji* 38% silk, 25% cotton, 22% rayon/viscose, 15% nylon; 50g (1.75oz); 115m (125yds)

BERROCO *Lago* 81% rayon/viscose, 19% linen; 50g (1.75oz); 94m (103yds)

BERROCO *Linsey* 64% cotton, 36% linen; 50g (1.75oz); 104m (114yds)

CLASSIC ELITE YARNS/JIL EATON *CottonTail* 100% cotton; 50g (1.75oz); 82m (90yds)

FIESTA YARNS *Ballet* 50% superfine alpaca, 50% tencel; 113g (4oz); 229m (250yds)

KNIT ONE, CROCHET TOO *Babyboo* 45% bamboo, 55% nylon; 50g (1.75oz); 105m (115yds)

MANOS DEL URUGUAY *Silk Blend* 70% extrafine merino wool, 30% silk; 50g (1.75oz); 137m (150yds)

Light

5–5.5 knit stitches to 1"

18–20 WPI

WPI *The plain, balanced weave sett (ends per inch, EPI and picks per inch, PPI) for most yarns is equal to half the wraps per inch (WPI). See page 23.*

weave • knit • wear

3

continued

ROWAN *Felted Tweed DK* 50% merino wool, 25% alpaca, 25% viscose; 50g (1.75oz); 175m (191yds)

TWISTED SISTERS *Essential* 60% hemp, 40% silk; 50g (1.75oz); 123m (135yds)

4

Medium

4–4.5 knit
stitches
to 1"

16–18 WPI

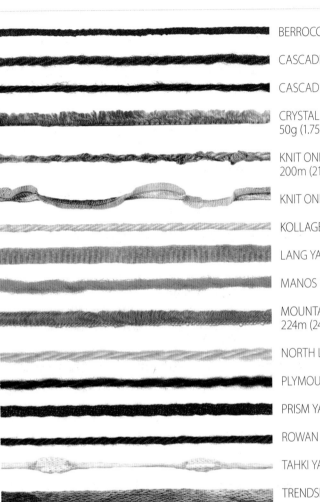

BERROCO *Captiva* 60% cotton, 23% polyester, 17% acrylic; 50g (1.75oz); 90m (98yds)

CASCADE YARNS *Cascade 220* 100% Peruvian Highland wool; 100g (3.5oz); 200m (220yds)

CASCADE YARNS *Pure Alpaca* 100% baby alpaca; 100g (3.5oz); 200m (220yds)

CRYSTAL PALACE YARNS *Aria* 38% rayon, 35% merino wool, 18% polyester, 9% nylon; 50g (1.75oz); 123m (134yds)

KNIT ONE, CROCHET TOO *Fleurtini* 34% wool, 26% cotton, 34% acrylic, 6% nylon; 100g (3.5oz); 200m (219yds)

KNIT ONE, CROCHET TOO *Tartelette* 50% cotton, 50% nylon; 50g (1.75oz); 69m (75yds)

KOLLAGE YARNS *Riveting Worsted* 100% recycled blue jeans; 100g (3.5oz); 149m (163yds)

LANG YARNS *Sol Dégradé* 100% cotton; 100g (3.5oz); 197m (217yds)

MANOS DEL URUGUAY *Wool Clasica* 100% wool; 100g (3.5oz); 126m (138yds)

MOUNTAIN COLORS *Merino Ribbon* 80% superfine merino wool, 20% nylon; 113g (4oz); 224m (245yds)

NORTH LIGHT FIBERS *Worsted* 100% baby alpaca; 106g (3.75oz); 123m (135yds)

PLYMOUTH YARNS *Baby Alpaca Worsted* 100% baby alpaca; 50g (1.75oz); 93m (102yds)

PRISM YARNS *BonBon* 100% rayon; 56g (2oz); 80m (88yds)

ROWAN *Handknit Cotton* 100% cotton; 50g (1.75oz); 85m (93yds)

TAHKI YARNS *Ripple* 100% mercerized cotton; 50g (1.75oz); 130m (142yds)

TRENDSETTER YARNS *Orchidea* 42% cotton, 42% acrylic, 16% nylon; 50g (1.75oz); 82m (90yds)

TRENDSETTER YARNS *Phoenix* 66% viscose, 34% cotton; 50g (1.75oz); 92m (101yds)

TRENDSETTER YARNS *Twiggy* 47% linen, 32% viscose, 21% polyamide; 50g (1.75oz); 78m (**85yds**)

TRENDSETTER YARNS *Zoe* 50% cotton, 45% viscose, 5% polyester; 50g (1.75oz); 69m (75yds)

5

Bulky

3–3.5 knit
stitches
to 1"

10–14 WPI

PAGEWOOD FARM *Silk Ribbon* 100% silk; 227g (8oz); 31m (34yds)

TRENDSETTER YARNS *Kinetic* 45% wool, 33% polyamide, 22% acrylic; 100g (3.5oz); 85m (93yds)

135

Yarn suppliers

Berroco *www.berroco.com*
Borgs *www.borgsvavgarner.se*
Cascade Yarns *www.cascadeyarns.com*
Classic Elite Yarns *www.classiceliteyarns.com*
Claudia Hand Painted Yarns *www.claudiaco.com*
Crystal Palace Yarns *www.straw.com*
DMC *www.dmc.com*
Fiesta Yarns *www.fiestayarns.com*
Habu Textiles *www.habutextiles.com*
Knit One, Crochet Too *www.knitonecrochettoo.com*
Kollage Yarns *www.kollageyarns.com*
Manos del Uruguay *www.fairmountfibers.com*
Mountain Colors *www.mountaincolors.com*

North Light Fibers *www.northlightfibers.com*
Pagewood Farm *www.pagewoodfarm.com*
Plymouth Yarn *www.plymouthyarn.com*
Prism Yarns *www.prismyarn.com*
Redfish Dyeworks *www.redfishdyeworks.com*
Rowan *www.knitrowan.com*
Silk City Fibers *www.silkcityfibers.com*
S. Charles Collezione *www.tahkistacycharles.com*
Tahki Yarns *www.tahkistacycharles.com*
Trendsetter Yarns *www.trendsetteryarns.com*
TSC Yarns *www.tahkistacycharles.com*
Twisted Sisters *www.twistedsistersknitting.com*

Online sources

Bag handles
Jul Designs *www.juldesigns.com*
Pacific Trims *www.pacifictrimming.com*

Buttons
One World Button *www.oneworldbuttons.com*
JHB *www.buttons.com*

Dress forms
PGM *www.allbrands.com*

Rigid-heddle looms and tools
Ashford Wheels & Looms
   www.foxglovefiber.com
Beka Inc *www.bekainc.com*
Bluster Bay *www.blusterbaywoodworks.com*
Glimakra USA *www.glimakrausa.com*
Harrisville Designs *www.harrisville.com*
Kromski *www.kromskina.com*
Lacis *www.lacis.com*
Le Clerc looms Inc *www.leclerclooms.com*
Schacht Spindle Co *www.schachtspindle.com*

Sewing machines - mini
Janome *www.homedepot.com*
Singer Pixie Plus *www.singerco.com*

Weaving and knitting yarns
Cotton Clouds *www.cottonclouds.com*
Eugene Textile Center
   www.eugenetextilecenter.com
Halcyon Yarn *www.halcyonyarn.com*
WEBS *www.yarn.com*
Websters *www.yarnatwebsters.com*
The Mannings *www.the-mannings.com*
Village Spinning & Weaving
   www.villagespinweave.com
Yarn Barn of Kansas *www.yarnbarn-ks.com*

Books on my shelf

A Treasury of Knitting Patterns and
A Second Treasury of Knitting Patterns
   Barbara G. Walker
   Schoolhouse Press, 1998
Creative Weaving
   Sarah Howard and Elisabeth Kendrick
   Lark Books, 2007
The Art of Weaving
   Else Regensteiner, Van Nostrand
   Reinhold, 1970
The Best of Weaver's Thick 'n Thin
   Madelyn van der Hoogt,
   XRX Books, 2001
The Handweaver's Pattern Directory
   Anne Dixon, Interweave Press, 2007
The Knitter's Handbook
   Rick Mondragon, Elaine Rowley,
   XRX Books, 2012
The Weaver's Idea Book
   Jane Patrick, Interweave Press, 2010
Weaving, A Handbook for Fiber Craftsmen
   Shirley E. Held, Holt, Rinehart and
   Winston, 1973

PROJECT INDEX

Heddle/reed width for largest size

5" width
Chiffon boa
Loopy scarf

10" width
Möbius cowl
Olive garden tunic

12" width
Sunshine jacket
The totes: Small tote
Three hats: Child's hat

15" width
Baby sack
Clutch
Pontunic
Summer dress whites
Three hats: Blue hat
              Log cabin hat

20" width
Aegean tunic
Bark cloth ruana
Be bold jacket
Big pockets jacket
Cleo's cover
Desert varnish
Field of pansies
Light & shade jacket
Liquid gold
Mad plaid jacket
Man vest
Moderne serape
Rag bag
Shawl-collared ruana
Sorbet jacket
The totes: Large tote
Tweedy shirt

Heddle/reed dents per inch

7.5/8-dent
Baby sack
The totes

10-dent
Aegean tunic
Bark cloth ruana
Be bold jacket
Chiffon boa
Mad plaid jacket
Man vest
Möbius cowl
Olive garden tunic
Rag bag
Sorbet jacket
Sunshine jacket
Three hats: Child's hat
              Log cabin hat

12/12.5-dent
Big pockets jacket
Cleo's cover
Clutch
Desert varnish
Field of pansies
Light & shade jacket
Liquid gold
Loopy scarf
Moderne serape
Pontunic
Shawl-collared ruana
Summer dress whites
Three hats: Blue hat
Tweedy shirt

Weaving only

Bark cloth ruana
Be bold jacket
Chiffon boa
Desert varnish
Field of pansies
Liquid gold
Loopy scarf
Möbius cowl
Pontunic
Rag bag
Shawl-collared ruana
Sorbet jacket
Tweedy shirt

Weaving and knitting

Aegean tunic
Baby sack
Big pockets jacket
Cleo's cover
Clutch
Light & shade jacket
Mad plaid jacket
Man vest
Moderne serape
Olive garden tunic
Summer dress whites
Sunshine jacket
The totes
Three hats

Acknowledgments

Putting together this book has been an amazing creative journey for me as well as a rewarding collaborative experience. There are many people I would like to thank.

My mom, for instilling in me a creative fashion sense, and for teaching me how to knit, crochet, and sew a hem.

My dad, for believing in me when I quit my *real* job to become a weaver?!?

Elaine Rowley and Rick Mondragon, for believing in the value of this project, and for your encouragement from conception to this beautiful finale. It was a bit of a rocky start, but your vision carried me through.

Alexis Xenakis, for your inspired photography.

Karen Bright, Managing Editor, for all of your assistance along the way.

The XRX staff, for your attention to details, details, details.

Madelyn van der Hoogt, for your clear eye at the end of the day, that helped pull it all together.

Cindy Howard-Gibbon from Foxglove Fiberarts Supply/Ashford Looms and Jane Patrick from Schacht Spindle Company, for your support of my work with rigid-heddle looms and for saying, "Here, try mine!" A very special thanks to Cindy. Your early-on appreciation of my work helped to keep me going.

The yarn companies, who supported this book by sending yarn — and then more yarn.

My friends, for your modeling services and encouragement along the way.

The weavers' guilds in Boston and Tucson, for providing me with a connection to the rare breed of people who are carrying on this craft. You provide inspiration, education, friendship, and affirmation that I am not alone. In particular, my friends from the Weavers' Guild of Boston and The Nashoba Valley Weavers' Guild who participated by contributing their fabulous weaving for the garments in the Gallery section. You are an inspiration!

And finally, my husband Steve Dyer, for keeping us fed and for your keen eye, good taste, and excellent editing abilities. We are forever interwoven.